Praise for
Faith, Farming, and Family

"*Moving, inspiring, real, raw, honest*... There are a thousand words I could use to describe *Faith, Farming, and Family,* but nothing will compare to what you feel as you read Caitlin's faith-filled words. She gets real and vulnerable where the rest of the world won't. Caitlin sheds light and biblical truth on her struggles and brings them back to Jesus every time. This book will change your life and outlook on it."

—Terryn Drieling, *Faith Family and Beef* (blog)

"Through everyday lessons from life on a farm, Caitlin speaks encouragement to our hearts. Her warm and relatable style invites you in as she shares both the trials and the triumphs of marriage, motherhood, and faith. From checking fences to feeding cows, Caitlin's stories will bring smiles and tears as she writes words of hope, ultimately pointing to the source of all hope—Jesus. Sharing about both the valleys of worry and fear and the mountaintops of love and new birth, Caitlin reminds each of us that God is always present and working to bring about wholeness, forgiveness, and redemption in our lives. *Faith, Farming, and Family* reads like a breath of fresh hope."

—Ginger Hughes, *No Mama's Perfect* (blog)

"Caitlin Henderson's book, *Faith, Farming, and Family,* grants us an up-close look into the world of farming. Her warm and inviting tone welcomes her readers to draw close. It's as if we join her with a cup of coffee on her porch to hear the lessons God has taught her through the goodness and difficulties of everyday life. Though their circumstances may differ, women will relate to the biblical principles woven throughout the book and find practical applications for cultivating a life of faith anchored in the unchanging character of God."

—Vivian Mabuni, speaker and author of *Open Hands, Willing Heart*

"*Faith, Farming, and Family* gives an authentic picture of Caitlin's life that leaves the reader feeling both understood and inspired. Caitlin dives into topics that any woman could relate to but might not yet have put words to. This book always points back to God's plan and reminds us that no matter where we find ourselves, He can bring beauty out of ashes."

—Kelli Bachara, *The Unraveling* (blog)

"In a world obsessed with more, more, more, Caitlin draws us back in with *Faith, Farming, and Family* and breathes life into the simple joys that help us experience God with a little more freedom and a lot more clarity."

—Amy Weatherly, cocreator of Sister, I Am with You

Faith, Farming, and Family

Faith, Farming, and Family

Cultivating Hope and Harvesting Joy
Wherever You Are

Caitlin Henderson

WATERBROOK

Faith, Farming, and Family

Published in the United States by WaterBrook, an imprint of Random House, a division of Penguin Random House LLC.

Library of Congress Cataloging-in-Publication Data
Names: Henderson, Caitlin, author.
Title: Faith, farming, and family : cultivating hope and harvesting joy wherever you are / Caitlin Henderson.
Description: First edition. | Colorado Springs : WaterBrook, 2021.
Identifiers: LCCN 2019054903 | ISBN 9780525654186 (hardcover) | ISBN 9780525654193 (ebook)
Subjects: LCSH: Henderson, Caitlin. | Farmers' spouses—Religious life—Kansas. | Farm life—Religious aspects—Christianity. | Rural families—Religious life—Kansas. | Mothers—Religious life—Kansas. | Christian life.
Classification: LCC BV4596.F3 H36 2021 | DDC 248.4—dc23
LC record available at https://lccn.loc.gov/2019054903

Printed in the United States of America on acid-free paper

waterbrookmultnomah.com

2 4 6 8 9 7 5 3 1

First Edition

For Jake:
You are God's greatest gift to me
and my very best friend.
I love you most.

For Grady, Porter, and Finley:
I am so thankful God chose me
to be your momma.
You are brave; you are strong;
you are loved.

Contents

Welcome to the Farm

I know that as you're reading this, you aren't actually at our farm. But if I had my way, we would be sitting on my farmhouse front porch, watching a beautiful Kansas sunset. We would skip the small talk, and we would get down to the good stuff. We would talk about life, motherhood, faith, and so much more.

As we sipped our coffee and watched the cattle graze in the pasture and the sun dip behind the trees, I would share my story with you. I would bare a vulnerable heart in the hope that you might relate and feel less alone and that you'd be encouraged to step into the person you were created to be. But since we aren't actually on the front porch, I'll share my heart with you here in these pages and pretend we are.

I'm Caitlin, but most people around here call me Mom or honey. I'll let you choose. I grew up in rural America but was still a town girl. I fell in love with a farm boy named Jake, so I took his last name, and we now have three little farm kids running around. Our two boys are Grady and Porter, and our little girl is Finley.

This way of life didn't come easily for me, and as I looked back on my years on the farm, I realized something beautiful. I could see clearly how God had taken many experiences from our farm and used them to mold me. I saw how He brought lessons out of each moment and used them to guide me. I believe He does that for you, too, even if your stories involve significantly less dirt and fewer tractors.

Often we live life in a daze. We go through the same motions and jam-pack our schedules, and something tragic happens. We are so busy getting through life, we forget to stop and savor the simple beauty right in front of us. The joy that comes from the simplest of life's moments is passed by as we keep pushing forward at full steam. It can be so easy to forge ahead and miss the lessons that were ingrained deep within these moments. We don't stop to look back and see the way God has woven all things together. We forget to pause and notice God's redemption in the chapters of our stories and the ways He has woven Himself into each page. But what if we dared to no longer settle for missing out on the simple beauty of life? What if we looked back in awe as we saw what God has done?

It took marrying a farm boy from Kansas and raising a family in rural America for me to realize all I was missing by trying to keep up with the unrealistic expectations society has set for us. God used simple yet valuable lessons from my life on the farm to show me there is more to life right here in this moment. Whether you are in the middle of a wheat field or in the heart of a city, together we can grab hold of these moments.

In these pages, I'm bringing you into my rural way of life. The big moments, the small moments, and everything in between. Each chapter creates a picture of how God can use the most ordinary things—even life on a farm—to show His character and goodness. The chapters reveal that no matter who we are or how we struggle, God wants us and He wants to use us.

I hope that as you read these pages, you'll realize the beauty of life right in front of you and find the hope, drive, and encouragement to take the next step—even if it's your first step—into bravely going where God is calling you.

I pray that as you begin to feel a desire to draw closer to God, you'll give up good in exchange for great and be able to savor the abundant joy that comes when we step into all God has for us.

I hope that this book is our conversation on the porch. That you picture yourself next to me on a porch swing as you tell me the dreams God has placed in the deepest corners of your heart. That your eyes open to the lessons you've learned throughout life and the ways your story has been written. And as you bravely share your vulnerable heart, I pray that you'll hear me say, "Go for it, sister! You can do it! I believe in you."

Faith, Farming, and Family

1
Shark Week Has Nothing on Cows
Learning to Face Your Fears

I just knew this was the day I was going to be killed. I stood paralyzed in fear, rationalizing my terror with a statistic—*There are more people killed by cows every year than by sharks*—and I knew I was going to be one of those people. As the moos grew louder, so did the pounding of my heart.

One day early in our marriage, my husband, Jake, ended up in bed with the flu. I don't mean the "man flu," where he really just had some sniffles but thought he was dying. No, this time he was extremely sick, the sickest I had ever seen him. I looked out our bedroom window at the frost on the branches and the clouds moving in with a winter storm. And I looked at my husband huddled under the covers and knew there was no chance he could get out of bed.

The words came out of my mouth—"Stay in bed. I'm

going to go feed the cows for you"—and I instantly regretted them. I was really hoping he would put up more of a fight, but I think the fever had made him somewhat delirious. Sure, I had ridden with him dozens of times to feed the cows, and I knew what and how much to feed them, but I was not confident in my ability to do it alone. I had become accomplished at opening and closing gates, and that was about it. I was far more comfortable sitting happily in the warm truck, smitten with my handsome farmer as he was busy out in the cold, feeding his "girls."

I hadn't grown up around cattle as Jake had. I had gazed at them from a distance while driving down our country roads, but that all changed when Jake and I started dating. I needed to know what I was getting into if I was going to become a farm wife, and cows were included in that mix. I always tried to play it cool, but I could climb a fence in a hot second if a cow even looked at me the wrong way. I had seen how angry a momma cow could get, and I knew the damage a 1,300-pound animal could cause.

I pulled on my coveralls and boots that frosty morning and climbed up into his big diesel truck. As I drove to the pasture where we kept our round hay bales, I gave myself a pep talk: "I've done this plenty of times with Jake. There's no difference. He's going to be so proud of me." I'm obviously great at pep talks.

I grabbed the remote that controlled the bale bed and

turned it on, double-checking to make sure I hadn't pushed the wrong button. I had used the bale bed before and knew I needed to back straight up to the hay bale, use the remote to lower the two metal arms on the pickup bed, squeeze the bale with the arms, and use them to lift the bale onto the pickup bed. I watched in the mirror as I held the button and the arms lifted the bale of hay onto the back of the truck with ease. Step one was accomplished without a hitch.

My confidence was rising as I drove the few miles to the pasture where the cows were. I hopped out of the truck, grabbed the icy metal of the gate, and swung it open so I could drive into the pasture. I turned to head back to the truck, and just when the thought crossed my mind that maybe I'd be okay after all, it happened.

I saw the cows heading for me and the opened gate, so I hurriedly jumped in the truck, pulled into the pasture, hopped out of the truck to shut the gate, and hopped back in the truck. The cows had heard the truck pull into the pasture, and they knew it meant dinnertime. Sixty momma cows came running and surrounded the truck, loudly sounding their dissatisfaction that I was taking so long to deliver their meal. I opened the door and sank in the mud as I hit the ground. I froze.

Cows kill more people than sharks. That fact rang in my mind, and I contemplated my options. Giving up wasn't an option. The cows had to be fed, and there was no way

Jake could do it. More than that, though, my pride was not about to admit defeat. So I got clever. I still wonder whether any neighbors or people driving by saw what happened next, but I doubt it or I would have become a viral sensation on the internet.

I unstuck my boots from the mud, stepped up on the running board, and contemplated my next move. When Jake fed the cows, he would walk through the herd to the back of the truck, lower the bale of hay to the ground using the bale bed, and cut the net wrap that holds the bale together. I didn't walk to the bed of the truck and do what Jake did. I stared at the large, demanding cows surrounding the truck, stretching their necks to try to sneak a nibble of hay, and I became paralyzed with fear. So I climbed *on top of* the truck. I crawled across the roof, trying not to slide off, as an entire herd of cows mooed and probably wondered why this crazy lady wouldn't just feed them already. I then climbed down onto the bed to cut the net wrap off and lower the bale to the ground. Only then did I realize I had left the remote that controls the bale bed in the center console of the truck. I had no way to lower the bale.

Maybe most people would have realized they were being a little dramatic. Maybe they would have just hopped down and walked to the cab to get the remote. They wouldn't have let their fear win. But not me. I climbed back onto the roof, scooted my way to the still-open door, shimmied down and got the remote, and reversed the process to get back to the bed. My nervousness grew, along with the impatience of the cows. I was in no danger where I was, yet my hands shook and my heartbeat pounded in my ears as I tried to finish the task. The cows were done waiting for me and were reaching over to eat the hay straight off the truck.

I cut the net wrap off the bale, lowered the bale to the ground, and proudly climbed back onto the roof, over to the door, and into the driver's seat. Mission accomplished. Now, I have to be honest: I don't think anyone knew that full story since I've never told the details until now. I have admitted to climbing onto the bed, but I don't think even Jake knew I climbed onto the roof. Because on the other side of my fear, I could see the irrationality of my actions in that situation. I was embarrassed by the fear that had gripped me. I threw logic out the window and let fear lead the way.

We are constantly faced with fear in this life, and every instance will require a choice from us, whether that fear comes from chasing our dreams, doing what God called us to do, or feeding cows. Although I got the job done, I used ten times the amount of effort I needed to as I danced around the situation instead of just facing the fear head on. Fear does one thing: it prevents us from living the lives God has called us to. It stops us in our tracks and keeps us from continuing to move forward in what God has planned for us.

Being scared of feeding the cows felt like a small inconvenience with few repercussions. But when I zoomed out and looked at the bigger picture, I realized that this fear of the cows could control a huge portion of my life as a farmer's wife. One seemingly silly fear could have stopped me in my tracks and done so much damage. It's the little lies we believe and the fears we have that Satan uses to distract and direct us. The impact those little things can have on us is wildly disproportionate. So many of our decisions are directed by fear: what we eat, how we parent, how we step out in faith, where we go. Our lives are constantly being led by fear. We let it slow us and stop us. Sometimes we become almost comfortable with it. We grow used to it and begin to no longer see the severity of it.

What is the fear that has power over your decision-making? The fear that feels like life or death? The fear you would rather exhaust your energy trying to dance around than face head on? We have a choice to either continue this dance or use the tools God has given us to fight for the life He is calling us to. Will we put our effort into avoiding our fears or facing them?

God says to us, "Have I not commanded you? Be strong and courageous. Do not be afraid; do not be discouraged, for the Lord your God will be with you wherever you go" (Joshua 1:9). We tend to think that overcoming fear is a good suggestion, something we'll get to later. We forget that God doesn't suggest being strong and courageous; He commands it. It is that important. He knows that day after day we will be presented with our fears, but He is reminding us that He will be alongside us in the midst of them.

These days, after years as a farmer's wife, I can feed the cows without climbing onto the roof of the truck. But I had to keep facing my fear until it no longer owned me. I had to go through the actions even when my insides felt as if they were going to burst. I had no option but to work through it. Saying I would try again tomorrow rather than facing it today only gave the fear more time to tighten its grip on me. Letting fear win once begins a ripple effect. Its hooks in us sink deeper every time we choose fear over faith. I can still climb a pasture fence faster than anyone, but I have become much braver through the years because I refuse to let fear control the path of my life. Your fear is probably different from mine, but I can bet that whatever it is has stopped you from being all in on the life God has planned for you.

When You Need a Push

I sat at a conference with forty other women as we went around the tables, listing our biggest fears pertaining to our dreams. My heart ached as I listened to the fears that were slowing and stopping those women: fear of failure, fear of success, fear of being vulnerable, fear of losing everything, fear of looking like an outcast. They all had one thing in common. Each woman's fear was stopping her from being all in on the dream God had placed in her heart. It was stopping her from living out God's will for her, and it was holding her prisoner to the lies she was believing. Fear places us exactly where the Enemy wants us. It leaves us powerless and cowering. It is our admission of defeat.

But conquering fear once doesn't mean it's gone forever. No, it's a constant war. It tries to sneak back in when we have our backs turned, and before we know it, we are shackled by its chains once again. John 14:27 says, "Peace I leave with you; my peace I give you. I do not give to you as the world gives. Do not let your hearts be troubled and do not be afraid."

We have to constantly be on guard and armed with the Word of God to remind us who we are and to whom we belong. We have to recognize the fear for what it is—a tool used by the Enemy to stop us—and we have to take the first step anyway. We need to remember that when we have faith, we will also have the peace that comes from God.

As I sat at that conference, I shared how God had once again put on my heart to host a weekend conference for farm wives called Fellowship on the Farm. I had held one two years prior but hadn't again since having our third baby. I struggled to host that first conference because I didn't feel worthy. The fear that no one would come—or, worse, that women would come and it would go horribly—constantly assaulted my mind. I didn't believe that God could use me to reach other women's hearts, and I wasn't sure I could be that vulnerable.

I shared how God so clearly laid before me every detail of Fellowship on the Farm and what a massive success it had been. Many of the women left in tears after hugging me and telling me that Fellowship on the Farm changed their lives. God moved in a huge way that weekend, and though my goal had been to bless those women, I had been immensely blessed in return. He had used my struggles and trials to help other women and bring Him glory.

So, I told the ladies at my table that I felt God was asking me to do it again. I told them that the month prior, for ten straight days, a different person each day brought up Fellowship on the Farm. Some were previous attendees, some were women who'd wanted to attend but couldn't, and some weren't even farm wives but were women who had heard about it. My husband told me that God was going to smack me upside the head if I didn't listen; clearly, He was trying to get my attention.

I knew without a shadow of a doubt that God was calling me again to host Fellowship on the Farm. Yet despite His clear call, still I doubted my worth. I let fear tell me I wasn't good enough and smart enough to pull it off a second time. It took my friend Terryn, who was also at my table, to snap me out of it. She steered me back to the biblical principles of obedience and trust. I reminded myself that I alone am not enough, that on my own I can do nothing, but that God put those dreams in my heart and could bring them to fruition through my obedience.

We've Got to Face the Fear

When God calls us to anything, we are going to be faced with fear. I don't mean the righteous fear of the Lord that gives us wisdom and keeps us humble, reminding us that we are clay in the Potter's hands. No, I mean the nasty fear from the devil himself that thwarts our righteous desires and actions. I believe it's one of the Enemy's greatest tools against us. God wants to use every aspect of our lives—our motherhood, careers, hopes, and dreams—for His glory and honor. What better way can the Enemy steal that plan than to make us afraid?

God knew we would struggle with this, and He gave us all the encouragement and truth we would need to go to battle. More than eighty Bible verses include the command to not be afraid. Matthew 10:28 takes that command a step further, as we are told to fear not those who can kill the body but the One who can kill the soul. Anytime I am really struggling with fear and I feel anxiety start to take over, I remember that verse, and I also go to the book of Esther. Esther is one of my favorite examples of choosing to face fear, even with the possibility of mortal consequences.

Esther was a Jewish orphan raised by her cousin Mordecai. When the king of Persia was looking for a new queen, Esther quickly won his favor. She became the queen while keeping her Jewish nationality a secret. So, when the king's right-hand man put into motion a plot to slaughter the entire Jewish populace throughout Persia, Esther had to make a choice—one that was fraught with danger. Fear stared her in the face, waiting for a decision.

She could take the safe road and keep her secret hidden. She could stay silent and remain unharmed while the Jewish people throughout the Persian Empire were slaughtered. She could continue as queen, never saying a word, and just suffer on the inside while her people perished.

Or she could face her fear and try to save her people in order to follow the path God had set before her. Approaching the king, however, involved risk to her position and her life. Explaining her plea for him to call off the massacre would mean admitting the truth of her own ethnicity, and King Xerxes was known for his hot temper.

But Esther had a person in her life to remind her that she was in her queenly position for a purpose. She had someone who, instead of just telling her what she wanted to hear, pointed her to the biblical truth that we are to be obedient when God calls us. Her cousin Mordecai reminded her that God can make a way without us, but what a sad day it is when He has to go to someone else because we were too afraid to allow Him to work through us. Mordecai encouraged her to choose faith over fear, even in the face of unfathomable danger. Esther chose faith, and despite her dangerous actions, her life was spared, as were her people.

While you and I might be tempted to discount the ways God asks us to step outside our comfort zones when we hear stories like Esther's, it is important to remember that every act of following God's call is important kingdom-building work. Giving in to fear, whatever we're being asked to do, causes us to miss opportunities to take part in God's redemption here on earth.

When God asks me to be vulnerable every day about my struggles and shortcomings in order to bring Him glory, I want to say no. Fear tries to tell me I'm opening myself up to criticism and hurt, my story can't be used, and God doesn't want me. And when I click the Publish button on a blog post and put my faults and struggles out into the world, I know I am inviting criticism.

But I also know it's worth it when the messages start pouring in from wives and moms who thought they were alone. Their hearts were touched, and they felt a little less alone because I refused to let fear win. I am reminded that pouring into women the truth that God loves them and made them for a purpose is worth the vulnerability. I am encouraged to believe that God is using me to help restore their hearts and refill their cups with truth and love. But I have come very close to telling God no because of the fear of failing.

I wish I could tell you that I'm a warrior against fear and that you can be too. I wish I could give you the end of this story: how I always look fear in the face and march right on. But I can't. Sometimes I let fear win, and sometimes I try to take the long way around. I climb on top of trucks and do anything I can to avoid facing it.

I've also learned over the years that we never regret letting God use us. When God calls us, that doesn't mean our paths will be painless or easy; it just means they're worth it. It is always worth it to choose faith over fear. We won't get it right every time, but that's why we have grace. We can let Him pick us up off the ground and dust us off, and we can try again tomorrow.

So, what are you facing today? What fear tugs on your heart and won't let go? What is the dream God has tucked into the depths of your soul that sounds too big and scary to accomplish? What situation are you in that is requiring you to be courageous and to trust the One who wants to use you for His glory?

I'm going to be that friend who reminds you of the

truth you already know: God wants to use you, but you have the free will to tell Him yes or no. He wants you to face that fear so you can get to the other side and experience what a life of freedom in Christ really means. He wants to work in your life and be the light that shines through you. He wants you to be obedient because He knows best and He knows your path. But you have to choose. Isaiah 35:4 says,

> Say to those with fearful hearts,
> "Be strong, do not fear;
> your God will come,
> he will come with vengeance;
> with divine retribution
> he will come to save you."

Today I encourage you to take the first step into whatever God is leading you to do. Is He asking you to start a business venture, take a mission trip, stay home with your babies, or tell the person in the grocery store about Jesus? Write down the scriptures from this chapter and hang them where you can see them often, or highlight or bookmark them in this book. And every time the Enemy tries to stop you from walking in your calling, go to those scriptures and arm yourself with truth.

You have to stand up and say you will no longer let fear rule your life and you'll face it head on until it no longer has power over you. You have to face it every day as a wife, mother, friend, daughter, and Christian. You have to take action, even when you're scared. You have to walk where God has asked you to walk, even when you feel as if you could burst. You have to refuse to let fear leave its hooks in you any longer. You have to pull on your boots and feed the cows.

2
Loosening the Reins
Learning to Give Up Control

My fury grew with every second that ticked by. I burned with hurt, brokenness, and anger, the kind of anger that brings tears to your eyes and makes you clench your jaw so tight that it aches. I had spent two hours preparing one of my husband's favorite meals, and two hours after he said he'd be home, his supper sat cold on the counter. I couldn't wait for him to walk in that door so I could let him have it. I was ready to fight.

His audacity and rudeness in showing up two hours late deserved my wrath, and I wasn't going to hold back. He knew I was making this meal for him as an act of love, and his lack of effort to get home was a dagger in the heart. It didn't matter whether his tardiness was out of his control; my brokenness longed to point its finger, and my husband was my target.

I had held the children off from the food as if I were fending off hungry raptors from their prey.

"Let's wait for Daddy to get home before we eat," I pleaded. But thirty minutes into the wait, I dished up their plates as I tried to swallow my annoyance. Another half hour passed, and I decided I would eat my supper. Except by that point, I was so angry I no longer had an appetite. With every minute that ticked by, my fury grew hotter and the food grew colder.

God help that man, I thought as I heard the gravel under his tires in the driveway. I contemplated whether I would meet him outside to give him a piece of my mind or just give him the cold shoulder for the rest of the night and let him try to beg for mercy. Whatever option I chose, he was going to know without a shadow of a doubt just how mad I was. I wanted him to feel the same brokenness I felt.

This story isn't a fun one to tell. To let the world know of our greatest insecurities, faults, and shortcomings is no easy task. You may read this and pick a side. Maybe you've been the wife who couldn't give grace to her husband when he came home late from work. Maybe you have walked in my shoes and understand where I'm coming from. You understand my longing for a simple family supper and the pain that came from the broken plan.

Or maybe you can clearly see my husband's case. You

feel sympathy toward him for working his hardest, only to come home to a bitter, cold wife. You are able to reason that things happen that are outside our control, and you let those things roll off your back. I admire you for that. I long for the ability to roll with the punches without my stomach twisting into knots. But on this night when my home-cooked meal sat untouched on the counter, I still thought I had control. I thought I was capable of being the one in charge, able to keep our family balanced and happy.

I didn't care what logical explanation was about to walk through that back door, because I didn't want to hear it. I had planned our evening, and now those plans were shattered. He had been working until well after dark for the last several weeks, and I was tired. I was tired of being lonely, and my fuse was short. Nothing could have justified the night I deemed ruined.

I chose the cold-shoulder method, in case you're wondering. I stood at the sink and glared out the window as I listened to the creak of the door opening and closing and the thud of his boots hitting the floor as he slipped them off. With each step I heard him take down the hallway, I tried not to explode. I glanced at the plate of chicken-fried steak with all the fixings, now dried out and cold. I had tried to keep it warm, but after two hours, it just wasn't going to taste the same. And by that point, I was glad it was cold. Tears of frustration tried to fall, but I tried even harder to hide them. My rage escaped in the form of frantically scrubbing grease out of the frying pan.

When I heard him step into the kitchen, I didn't even turn around. He could feel the anger radiating off me. "I'm sorry," he said in a defeated tone. "That heifer needed help, and I ended up having to pull that calf." I'd spent the last two hours being miserable because of unmet expectations while my husband had spent them out in the cold, trying to save a momma cow and her calf. I had spent those hours pacing my kitchen, and he had spent them doing everything he could to save two of our animals from death.

I wish this was the point in the story when I could tell you that I turned around and hugged my farmer, proud that he had just saved two lives. I wish I could say that I put his plate in the microwave, got him something to drink, and told him I loved him. That I took his coat, covered in manure, amniotic fluid, and blood, and threw it in the wash while he played with the kids. I wish.

Do two things clash in this world more than being a farmer's wife and a control freak—both of which I am? I thrive on organization, schedules, and all things type A personalities love. I want to know what is going to happen and when it's going to happen. I want to have my days and weeks planned and set in ink in my day planner. I want to be able to control what is happening around me and make sure things go predictably and smoothly. It's what keeps me sane and keeps our family on track. But it's also what almost ruined me.

Planning and being organized aren't all bad. But when things spin out of control, I am a mess. My anxiety spirals, and it completely overwhelms me. I am a much happier wife and mother when I feel as if I have life somewhat organized at least. But when I place control at the top of the list, it becomes a problem. When the control I need turns into an idol and I cling to it for comfort, I have an issue. Once I feel like I have control of something small, I keep grasping for more until I need control of all things. I become unable to draw a line in the sand and am quickly buried beneath the overwhelming emotions of not being able to juggle everything.

The problem with my unmet expectations was that they felt fully justified. They felt righteous. My emotions were my dictator. I didn't want to hear about his day or what he had been doing, because I was too busy wallowing in my bitterness. I wanted him home in time for supper, and there was no going back to make that happen. The bar had been set in my head for the way I thought our evening should go, and he had fallen short. I wanted to eat supper as a family and have an actual conversation with my husband without one of us falling asleep midsentence out of pure exhaustion. I wanted him to feel the hurt he had caused me to feel. I thought that pawning off my brokenness on someone else would heal me.

For every apology he laid on the table, I threw back a jagged insult. Every "I'm so sorry, honey" that rolled from his lips met a hateful glare. I was so deep in the pit of my anger that even when I realized the foolishness of my behavior, it was too late to climb out. The weight of my pride kept me from acknowledging my actions and salvaging the rest of the evening. My problem with control wasn't just that I felt entitled to it; it was also the person I became when I felt I was losing my grip on it.

The root of the problem, though, wasn't a husband who was late for supper. That may have been where I planted my flag and even what I believed at the time, but that wasn't the actual issue. The problem was that I had plans and thought I had control. When my farmer got caught up in his unpredictable situation, it meant I lost control of the plans I had for our evening.

That's the problem with believing we're in control. Yes, obviously we are in control of some things. We can control our actions, the words we speak, and the way we respond to situations. I couldn't control that my husband was late for supper, but I could have controlled how I responded. It's when we try to take control of our entire lives—when we rip that away from the One who created us because we decide we know what's best for us and believe we can do a better job of directing our lives—that we move into dangerous territory.

It's a breeding ground for broken spirits and escalating

anxiety. Scripture gets twisted to suit our desires, and we guard the course of our lives as we tell God to leave it up to us. We believe we are entitled to complete control.

It's satisfying to feel as if we're in control. We believe we can direct our lives to play out as we think they should. We pull situation after situation into our hands, and before we know it, our wills are no longer in line with God's. We let Him watch from a distance as we flounder around, trying to juggle our entire lives. We exhaust ourselves as we become frustrated when, time after time, things don't go as we planned. We repeatedly feel defeated when the load becomes too heavy, and we blame God for giving us more than we can handle.

The truth is we can't handle any of this. We were never meant to control every aspect of our lives. We will never be satisfied because we will never be able to control the actions of others and because many situations are simply beyond our control. Trying to control everything isn't how we are supposed to live. The effort is futile and will only bring pain.

I don't want you to think I'm pointing my finger at you and telling you how to live while I sit over here with life figured out as I sip my latte. No, I'm a mess. And control has ruled my life for far too long. But loosening our grip on some of that control opens us up to letting God work in our lives. It requires being willing to welcome His will, even when we don't know what that may look like.

It's a hard thing to give up control (or the illusion of control). Where do we draw the line? What do we allow God to have, and what do we keep? In my experience, it's all or nothing. Picking and choosing what we control is a slippery slope. If we aren't fully surrendered, then we will slowly pick those burdens back up until we're right back where we started. How can we be the hands of Christ, free to do God's work, when our hands are too full of burdens that aren't ours to handle or aren't within our realms of influence?

I struggled with this for years. If you thought my response to my husband missing supper was bad, imagine my reaction when big things felt out of my grasp. When the rains our crops so desperately needed didn't come, when the calf we doctored in the bathtub at two in the morning didn't survive, or when our two-year-old fell ill and doctors said leukemia was the likely culprit. I was miserable, which caused the people around me to be pretty miserable too. I watched my children like a hawk, terrified that something unthinkable would happen to them. I would call my husband many times a day to make sure he hadn't been hurt at the farm with no one around to help. I thought that my control equaled safety, that if I just did enough, I could keep our lives on the track I thought they were supposed to be on. Our human flesh longs for safety, and we will go to great lengths to ensure it. But a false sense of control does not equal safety.

Hand Over the Burdens

The urge to be in control doesn't come just with being married to a farmer. No, unfortunately, I think this is something we all struggle with. Our intentions are good—to keep our families safe. Not only are we following our instincts, but living Christ-centered lives as God asks also requires a certain amount of self-control. Our hearts may be in the right place, but total control was never our burden to carry. The control I am referring to is the control that pushes God out and puts us in His place.

In April 2018, I came to a breaking point. The burdens piled on our backs were too heavy to continue carrying. Through the lens of my pain, all I could see were struggles and heartache ahead—a sick child, a failing market for crop prices, a record-breaking drought, and a strained marriage. It felt as if everything was slipping through my fingers, and the tighter I gripped, the more futile the effort. I had no power against the big trials that came crashing down around us, and the feeling of being defenseless overwhelmed me.

During the height of my anxiety, I remained fervent in prayer. I thanked God for the blessings He had given us. I prayed for others. I pleaded for healing for our son. I begged for the drought to end, and I prayed that He would bring peace to my heart and release me from my anxiety. I felt close to Him in prayer, but nothing was giving. On the outside, I looked put together, but on the inside, a war was raging.

Attempting to climb out of the pit was useless. I just couldn't get a grip since my hands were too full from trying to carry the weight of the world. I would lay down my burdens at the cross and, not five minutes later, pick them back up. I would entrust them to God for a few minutes and then rip them back because I didn't truly believe He could handle them better than I could.

So, on a cool spring morning, as my kids played in the living room, I went into our bedroom and locked the door. I hit my knees and sobbed into the carpet. I lay there and cried the kind of cry that comes with loud wails and snot pouring down your face. With puffy eyes and a heart in shambles, I told God I was done. The things in my life that I had zero power over had been holding me hostage. I told Him I was all in—no more keeping one foot in the door just in case He couldn't handle it all. I couldn't keep living as if I were the one truly in control. I had to be in or out because I was tired to my bones of trying to fight for control.

I was handing it all over to the One it belonged to in the first place. "Anything." I sobbed the word over and over again until I believed it in my heart. "You can have anything from me, God. No holding back any longer. My children, my husband, the farm, our possessions, our comfort, our safety—anything." Then I got up, dried my tears, and called my husband to tell him I had just given God permission to do anything in our lives—as if God needed permission. But it was progress.

Every day I prayed the word *anything*. Over and over, like a reminder to me and God that I still meant it. I kept expecting something big to happen. I kept going back to Proverbs 19:21: "Many are the plans in a person's heart, but it is the LORD's purpose that prevails." Was He going to tell us to sell the farm and become missionaries? Was He going to let my husband or one of my children die? It was almost laughable that I really felt as if I had held enough control that handing it over would make for some big response from God.

Day after day I waited for God to speak, to tell me the momentous act He had in store for me. Little did I know that the great act that came with saying "Anything" was me working on my own heart. It was focusing on my own bondage and scars and letting my heart be changed. It was being willing to say, "I'm here. Use me however You need." Saying "Anything" meant looking inward at myself first and foremost. It meant admitting that maybe I didn't have it all together as I had thought I did.

The Freedom in Surrender

Maybe you don't try to control everything like I did. But it's in our human nature, and I would bet we all have things we cling to for dear life, afraid to surrender. I'm not saying surrender is easy, but I am saying it's worth it. The things in this world that we can't control, big and small, suck up our time and energy as we try to direct them. The struggle makes us anxious and exhausted and turns our focus from what God calls us to. On the other side of surrender, however, is freedom and the ability to focus on God's commands instead of spending our energy focusing on the things we have no control over anyway.

The world we live in says that we are in control. It says that we can command our destinies and accomplish anything we set our minds to and that we should do only the things that make us happy. It's a message that's powerful and palpable, and it makes us feel good. But it isn't realistic or attainable, and it isn't what the Bible says. Proverbs 16:9 says, "In their hearts humans plan their course, but the LORD establishes their steps." Hard work can get you far, and God does place dreams and desires in our hearts. But when we remember that the two greatest commandments are to love the Lord our God and to love our neighbors as ourselves, it changes things. It means letting Him lead us but being willing to work toward whatever He may be calling us to do.

What situations are you clinging to? Are you clinging to the safety of your family so much that it has become your idol? Or maybe you're struggling with controlling the actions of those around you or situations at work or with friends. Maybe your desire for control runs so deep through your heart that your husband coming home late for supper makes you come unglued.

That one-word prayer—"Anything"—changed my life. It opened my heart to trust that the God of the universe can handle my life. It's a prayer I pray almost daily because if I don't constantly remind myself, I find my arms filling back up with burdens that should have been left at the cross. But letting go of the big stuff means we are also free and have more willpower to let go of the small stuff.

What would happen if you told God "Anything"? What would happen if you went into your bedroom, hit the floor, gave Him your whole heart, and quit trying to manipulate and direct the things you have no power over? What would happen if you quit putting your energy and emotions into trying to do your will but instead tried to do His?

I can tell you what would happen. You would have peace that passes all understanding (see Philippians 4:7). You would struggle with picking those burdens back up, but if you clung to that word—*anything*—then something would change. God might not loudly proclaim His mighty works, but maybe His tender whispers into your heart would shape radical change inside you.

And then that new heart He placed inside your chest would slowly pour out into the open. As you continued to humble yourself and open your hands to lay those burdens at the cross, you would be free to focus on His will and the calling He has given you. It is when we leave the burdens there that we are able to be at peace. We are able to go with the flow and be okay when situations don't go as planned. We are able to be more in the moment with our families, love God and love others as we are commanded, and do the work we have been called to do. We are able to let God lead us. We are able to allow ourselves to be the hands and feet of Christ. And if you're wondering, my husband still comes home late for supper quite a bit. But "Anything" means I'm okay with eating supper late—sometimes.

3

Stuck in the Muck

Learning as You Go

He leaned over and placed a quick kiss on my lips before climbing down off the tractor. As he walked away, he yelled back with a smile, "I'll be right back. Try not to get the tractor stuck!" With a flirty smirk, I assured him there was no need to worry. I had driven the tractor several times and was sure I'd be just fine.

I made my way back and forth across the field and remembered to pull the correct levers at the correct times, to watch my corners, and to not turn too sharply. I quickly became overconfident and tried to show off by swinging the tractor out toward the mud as Jake had been doing. I wanted him to see what a good job I could do and was hoping that when he got back to the field and saw my work, he would think, *Man, she'd make a good wife! I should put a ring on her finger!* I wanted to show him I was serious about joining him in this way of life.

But I got too close to the mud, and my heart dropped into my stomach as I felt the tractor sink. My eyes widened as I looked down and saw the tires spinning but going nowhere.

The more I tried to get unstuck, the deeper I sank. Jake had left his girlfriend and his teenage brother, Casey, to work a field while he ran to town to get parts, and he had no idea of the circus that was happening while he was gone. I knew I was about to eat crow as I waited for him to get back to the field. I laid my head down on the steering wheel and laughed, mostly so I didn't cry.

Casey and I hatched a plan. We thought that we could use the other tractor to pull mine out and that Jake would be none the wiser about our little mishap. Unfortunately, when Jake pulled into the field, not only one tractor was stuck in the mud but two. We stood there trying to stifle our giggles as we watched Jake try to figure out how we had gotten ourselves into that mess and how he was going to get us out of it.

Now, years later when we all get together, we sit around and laugh about all the predicaments we got ourselves into back then. I chuckle at all the times I failed miserably and did more harm than good. My cheeks turn red as I think about the number of times I let the cattle out or got something stuck in the mud. Looking back at those first years as a farmer's wife, I wonder how I made it through alive. I cringe as I think about how I awkwardly fumbled my way through each new role. It never fails that I still get something stuck at least once every year and have to make the dreaded SOS call to my husband to pull me out. At this point, I think getting things stuck in the mud is one of my spiritual gifts.

But don't we do that with so many aspects of our lives? We look back and think *Oh my heavens* as we remember how far we have come. We think about the petty fights in those first years of marriage, when being right was more important than having a happy marriage. As we serve up that beautiful lasagna, we think back to when cooking dinner without setting off the smoke detector was a victory. (Okay, maybe it still is sometimes. No shame.) We look at our lives now and compare them with when we became a wife or a mom or when we started our careers, and we think that if we only knew then what we know now, we could have done things so differently.

Maybe looking back is the easy part for you. You are okay with comparing yourself now with who you were then because you have more experience under your belt. You have grown in areas of your life and can look back and see that transformation over time so clearly. You can see that the struggles and awkwardness brought growth, so they were worth it. Your scars are reminders of your strength, and you're thankful for the lessons learned.

Or maybe looking back brings you pain. You would rather forget the mistakes you made and the times you stumbled. Looking back brings you shame, guilt, or embarrassment. You don't want to reflect on your past because bringing it up will do no good and there is no going back now, so what's the point?

But what about when we look forward, when we think about where we want to be in the future? What feelings rise to the surface when we think about where we are now compared with where we want to be? Do we still chuckle because we know we will probably have some mishaps on the way, or do we harshly judge our progress because we aren't as far as we wanted to be? Do we look at our past progress and future progress with the same attitude? Do we give ourselves grace for not having everything just right?

I wish I could sit down with you, hand you a cup of coffee, and tell you that you aren't perfect. Hear me out, friend. You are not a perfect wife, mother, Christian, friend, employee, business owner, or anything else. And neither am I. And neither is the woman on Instagram who looks as if she is—the one we keep comparing ourselves with because it looks as if she's got it all together.

You and I weren't called to be perfect. We weren't called to get everything right or to never stumble along the way. Not in anything we do. Setting those unrealistic expectations for ourselves is going to smother us. If we were perfect, there would have never been a need for the Cross. Of course, we should strive every day to be better than we were the day before, and we should want to continue to grow and learn. But we will never reach perfection. More than that, God never intended for us to wear ourselves out focusing on reaching perfection, because it will never happen.

We learn as we go in everything we do. In marriage, parenting, business, and everything else, we learn through experience. We do our best in the moment, but we continue to figure out what works and what doesn't. We constantly play the game of trial and error, and our strategies and skills evolve as we learn from our mistakes. We mess up, fumble the ball, and sometimes take a step backward. All of us.

So many of us beat ourselves up for not getting it right from the start, and then we get frustrated. We can look back and see how far we have come, but when we look forward, all we see are roadblocks that we think we will never get through. And as we focus on the muck and the hard stuff, we become anxious, thinking we have to do everything right this second.

We get caught in a vicious cycle of going from frantically trying to do everything perfectly to being completely burned out. We say we are going to drink enough water, stop yelling at our kids, keep our houses clean, cook homemade meals, and put on real pants . . . all in the same day. We get our hopes up that this is the time when it sticks, when we really turn our lives around and get it right.

All that does is set us up for failure and steal our joy. We last about two hours, if we're lucky, and at our first mistake, we throw in the towel and call it quits. We feel embarrassed for even believing this would be the time we stuck to our goals. We go from embarrassed to anxious and defeated, and we start the cycle all over again.

Flat Tires

I get messages from other farm wives who feel frustrated and defeated because they believe they aren't cut out for this way of life. They don't think they will ever find their purpose or grow accustomed to farm life. They judge themselves by their failures, and they don't believe that even years down the road they will get any of it right.

I love to tell them the story of a time when Jake and I were dating and I scraped up four miles of dirt road with the disc that's used to cultivate the ground before noticing anything was wrong. It was the first time I had to move the tractor from one field to another, and I was a nervous wreck. My hands were hot and sweaty, my heart was racing, and I thought I was going to pee my pants.

I was so focused on getting to the next field that I didn't notice I had blown not only one tire on the large piece of equipment I was pulling behind me but two.

Every few seconds I would glance back as I had been taught, but a section of the disc was blocking my view of the tires in the middle, and I never leaned over *quite* far enough to see them.

It wasn't until I was turning a corner that I could finally see the blind spot on the disc behind me, and I noticed I no longer had a tire on the middle rim. I had completely lost the tire a few miles back and had also been dragging the rim down the road the entire time, not only ruining the rim but also making a very obvious trail in the dirt road. The tire next to it was still on the rim but was completely flat.

I pulled the tractor into a field entrance, called Casey on the radio, and told him what happened. I asked him to call Jake and tell him because I was too scared to tell him myself. I had messed up big time, and I knew there was no way I could ever be trusted to help on the farm again. All I had managed to do was break things or get equipment stuck. Clearly, I was just not meant to be on a farm. This way of life was not for me.

At this point in our relationship, Jake and I had yet to have our first fight. I thought this was probably the day that would change that. Casey listened to my panic over the radio, and he tried to calm me down with jokes. I said, "Your brother is going to kill me!" and his reply was "Yeah, probably" as he laughed over the radio. Casey said he was tired of being the one to get corrected just because he wasn't as pretty.

I saw Jake's truck round the corner, come down the road, and pull up next to the tractor. He got out of his truck, and I thought about how sad it was that the last time I would see him, he would have to look so dang good. He grinned underneath his dusty ball cap and motioned for me to come down from the tractor.

I shook my head. *Nope, I'm not coming down from this tractor. I know I screwed up and I'm a liability. I'll just go home and pretend we never met.* He persisted, and I persisted more, refusing to face him. My cheeks burned with embarrassment, and I couldn't handle getting dumped right this moment by the man of my dreams.

Finally, when he realized I wasn't budging, he came to me. As he climbed up onto the tractor, I cursed the person who decided tractors didn't need to be locked from the inside. My heart beat faster as he reached to open the door of the cab. I buried my face in my hands, ready for what was coming. Instead, I heard laughter.

I popped my head up and looked him dead in the eye. "What's so funny?" I demanded to know. There was nothing about this situation that I could find humor in. He grinned with that infectious smile of his and said, "Well, it's no big deal. I'll fix it." He caught me in his arms as I jumped off the last step. As we drove to town to get two new tires, he glanced at me and gave me a wink, signaling me to take a breath.

See, if I had gotten my way that day, I would have quit. I would have done anything possible to avoid Jake and the embarrassment of failure. I would have washed my hands of the whole thing and never looked back. I would have walked back to town and given up. I'd have given up on helping on the farm and ever marrying a farmer. I thought it was painfully clear that I was not cut out for this.

But that isn't where my story ended, and wherever you are isn't the end of your story either. Jake took my hand and refused to give up on me when I thought I was hopeless, because he knew I just needed to learn as I went. He didn't expect me to know everything or get it perfect. He helped me take the next step when I was too afraid and believed in me when I didn't believe in myself.

My striving for perfection was tearing me up because I was working for the wrong reasons. I was trying so hard to show Jake how good I was that I had no time to focus on what God had to say. I cared about being perfect in the eyes of people more than in the eyes of my heavenly Father. Paul said in Galatians 1:10, "Am I now trying to win the approval of human beings, or of God? Or am I trying to please people? If I were still trying to please people, I would not be a servant of Christ."

To be fair, I'm a pretty good tractor operator these

days, but you'd better believe there isn't a day that goes by when I don't fail miserably at something. There isn't a day when I don't make a mistake or regret not doing something differently. I might have come a long way, but that doesn't make me perfect by a long shot. I've just learned not to take my mistakes too seriously. I've learned that it isn't my mistakes that define me; what matters is what I do after each mistake and how I can learn from it.

Most of the time I push through, take the lesson, and apply it, but sometimes I get stuck just as I did that day in the tractor. And sometimes I need someone to take my hand and help me take the next step forward. Sometimes I need the reminder that God says to keep persevering and that my lack of perfection should not be able to steal my joy. Sometimes I'm so focused on where I'm standing now that I forget to look back and see how far I've come.

Today let me be the person who reminds you of that. I will be the person who will gently push you to keep going. God isn't asking you for perfection, but He is asking you to strive to be more like Him. In whatever it is you're called to do or whatever season of life you're in, you will stumble. You will fail, but what matters is what you do next. What matters is your effort and heart and your willingness to keep going.

While you're beating yourself up about not being where you want to be, God is asking you to let Him keep working on you. Part of the beauty of life is continuing to learn and grow, no matter how old we are. As long as we are breathing, God wants to continue to use us. Isaiah 41:10 says,

> Do not fear, for I am with you;
> do not be dismayed, for I am your God.
> I will strengthen you and help you;
> I will uphold you with my righteous right hand.

If we shift our focus from cringing at our mistakes to viewing them as opportunities for learning and growth, then we can shift our perspective from our current condition to the ever-closer goal ahead. We can get up and do our best, knowing it won't be perfect. We can know that sometimes we are going to fall down and be dragged through the mud. We can stay there, or we can get back up.

We don't have to let our mistakes steal our joy, and this is coming from someone who is a recovering perfectionist. Let's stop beating ourselves up for the things we don't get right and instead focus on what we can do to keep looking more like His image. Let's keep putting one foot in front of the other as we learn not to take ourselves too seriously. Let's promise to give ourselves some grace when we fall down. Let's embrace our imperfection and view it as an opportunity for God to work in us. Let's get back up in the tractor and give it another go.

4

The Refiner's Fire

Learning to Be Strengthened in the Hard Times

The ringing grew louder and louder in my ears. My hands shook as adrenaline pumped through my body. My phone slipped from my hands as I buried my face in our toddler's pillow. I got up and paced the house, trying to find something to occupy myself. I thought if I could just clean or maybe bake something, my mind would stay busy enough that I wouldn't have to face reality. I needed to feel productive and needed. But there was no task I could complete because my hands shook relentlessly and my heart pounded in my chest as hot tears poured down my face.

Nothing could calm the rush of emotions that surged through me. Embarrassment turned into shame, which turned into anger, which turned into sadness, which turned back into embarrassment. A vicious cycle was quickly forming. Anger at my husband, at God, and at myself for having fallen in love with this life. I felt so small and helpless in the scheme of things. I was desperate. The adrenaline faded, and in its place a knot formed in the pit of my stomach.

My husband had devoted his entire life to the farm, and it was a family effort. It was where we had our first date, said our vows, and had some of our biggest fights. It was where we two-stepped on the dusty shop floor as an old country song played over the staticky speakers. It was where we had built our entire life. It had been entrusted to so many generations before him, and there we stood, six years after our wedding, as our banker said, "Sell the farm." Ours was the generation it was going to end with. I leaned against the doorframe, my eyes fixed on our children as they drove their tractors on the carpet, blissfully unaware of the way their lives were about to be altered. I ached at the thought of them not having the opportunity to carry this on.

I begged Jake for answers, for him to just tell me it was going to be okay. He was the one who was always strong. He was the one who kept it together for the rest of us. As I watched my husband break down, I was shattered and frightened. All we knew was the farm, and it was all we wanted. We wanted nothing more than to raise our children here, teaching them how to be stewards of God's land and animals.

We had nothing to fall back on. The last three years

had been full of challenges, but I kept expecting things to turn around. Surely our hard work would redeem the low markets and the hits of Mother Nature. We were going on year four of a horrible drought, and wheat prices had dropped to the lowest they had been in thirty years, while input costs remained high. We had done what we could, but it wasn't enough. We watched the For Sale signs pop up in fields of other farms, and the sight of those signs stirred a helplessness that couldn't be ignored.

Five generations had led to my husband. Five generations fought their way through depressions, droughts, dust bowls, insects, fire, hail, low commodity prices, and so much more. The phrase *blood, sweat, and tears* was literal for them. The weight of this legacy rested solely on our shoulders, and the pressure to succeed was daunting.

They handed the farm from one generation to the next, passing the baton and pouring into each what it meant to be a farmer. They lived and breathed this entire life in a way that can't be explained. In each generation, they instilled the values of hard work, stewardship, faith, humility, and love. And I felt incredibly privileged that Jake had taken my hand and brought me into this way of life with him. It had changed and shaped me in ways I never could have imagined.

When my husband was eighteen years old and fresh out of high school, his dad was killed in a car accident. Since he was the oldest child, the responsibility fell on his shoulders. Not much more than a child himself, he inherited a thousand-acre farm and the mountain of debt that came with it. He was thrown into the role of owner and operator just a week before harvest, the busiest time of year. In addition to dealing with the fresh pain of losing his father, he had to make huge financial and business decisions.

Three years later, we were married and tucked our heads to plow through and keep the farm successful. We grew the operation, expanded our herd of cows (and children), and were proud of the work we were putting in to keep this tradition afloat. This life of farming wasn't just a job for us—especially for my husband. It was a passion and love that ran five generations deep through his veins. It was a way of life that he couldn't fathom not living. He had been on that farm since the day he was born. There he had won dirt clod fights, chased fireflies, and learned the meaning of hard work. The farm had shaped him into the man he is.

And now here I stood at my kitchen sink as the news sank in that it could all be gone. I crumpled under the pressure. I tried to cling to the truth that God is good and His plans are greater than our own. I tried to stay positive and have hope, but I was angry. I was in the fire, and it was all I could see around me. I watched as our entire life started to crumble at the foundation. I begged God to just tell me what was going to happen to us. I wanted nothing more than to fast-forward to the end of this chapter to see how the story played out.

We were facing the hardest thing we had ever confronted as a family. We were in the wilderness, and we felt as if God had abandoned us. We knew other people out there had much bigger problems, and it wasn't lost on us that things could have been worse. But we were in a season of desperation, trying to fight our way through. We had no choice but to face the battle head on.

Jake began running himself ragged, diversifying in every way he could. He drove a semi, helped out neighbors here and there, and worked ridiculous hours to persuade the bank to hang on for a while longer. We pleaded our case, and they agreed to wait another year. They said that the amount of work Jake was doing to save the farm made them believe he could see it through. His work ethic had been unmatched, and it bought us time. But we were still hanging on by a thread, and now the kids and I saw Jake even less than we had before. Sometimes he worked three jobs in a single day and slept just a few hours when he could at random times.

When he left for two weeks to haul cotton, I stayed home and took care of all our cows even though I was eight months pregnant with our third child. Though the people at the bank were amazed at what we were doing, we didn't know how long we could keep it up. We were so tired.

I was exhausted to the core of my bones, and my fuse was short. My anxiety constantly bubbled at the surface, ready to overflow onto my family in the form of rage. I didn't think I could keep hanging on to this dream. I even tried to talk Jake into waving the white flag at one point. There were many hurt feelings, angry words, and slammed doors in those months.

Suffering Turns to Good

Our human instinct is to shy away from pain, to do anything possible to avoid the hurts and trials of life. No one asks to walk through the fire, but it is unavoidable. I sat at our dining room table as tears stained the pages of my Bible. I read Romans 5:2–5 and soaked in the words of the apostle Paul. I read them over and over until I had them tucked safely in my heart: "We boast in the hope of the glory of God. Not only so, but we also glory in our sufferings, because we know that suffering produces perseverance; perseverance, character; and character, hope. And hope does not put us to shame, because God's love has been poured out into our hearts through the Holy Spirit, who has been given to us."

There was no rejoicing in my sufferings. There was wallowing, blaming, and coldness of my heart. There were cries in the wilderness and hearing only the echo of my own voice. I didn't think I could persevere. I didn't have the hope I needed to pull me through. But it wasn't going to be my hope that pulled me through; it was going to be Jesus who walked the path with me, leading me step by step.

Even though I felt as if there were no light ahead, I kept that nugget of truth tucked safely away. When another bill came that we couldn't pay, I reminded myself of Paul's words. When another bill collector called, I clung to the truth I had been guarding inside me. When it all felt like too much, I leaned in closer to the comfort of those words.

I walked through the fire, clutching the only truths that could see me through to the other side. I tucked my head and put one foot in front of the other. I whispered Paul's words when just thinking them wasn't enough. I tried to turn my focus from the heat of the flames to the One who would see me through them. I couldn't rely on my own strength, ability, or smarts to get me out of the fire. I learned that the saying "God gives us only what we can handle" is a lie. I knew that without Him, I could handle none of what I was being dealt.

Then one day I noticed something. I lifted my chin, looked around, and realized that the fire wasn't quite as hot. Or maybe the fire was still raging, but Paul's words had changed me. Maybe my suffering really had turned into perseverance, and maybe my perseverance really had turned into character, which had turned into hope. Maybe the fire had changed me. Maybe the only way for me to truly be strengthened was to walk through the fire. Maybe the fire's purpose was not to consume me but to refine me.

Psalm 66:10–12 says,

> You, God, tested us;
> you refined us like silver.
> You brought us into prison
> and laid burdens on our backs.
> You let people ride over our heads;
> we went through fire and water,
> but you brought us to a place of abundance.

It isn't by the joys and times of ease that we are strengthened and refined but by the burdens and fires. It's in the unimaginably hot flames that we are changed and our hearts are molded.

Sometimes I still forget. Sometimes I rely more on myself than I do on God to see me through. When life is on a fairly normal path and we are in the thick of routines, I forget. I forget that the God of the universe is still in control. I forget that there is a picture bigger than what I can see. I turn to my own strength to see me through. I try to flip to the end of the chapter instead of reading each page, word for word. But then I remember who it is that sees me through the fires.

Today we are still hanging on by a thread, but the

thread is a little thicker. The pile of bills is still high, the stresses are abundant, and the banker is still on our heels. Things are no easier now than when we got that first call, but we've changed. Though the fire still rages, we know we don't walk through it alone. We know that whatever fire we are going to walk through will bring perseverance, character, and hope. We know we can let it go to waste or we can let it be redeemed and used for God's glory.

I'm thankful for that first step into those flames because they brought the refinement I needed to prepare me for what lay ahead. It was painful, and I didn't know whether I would come out on the other side. Some days I didn't know what our next step would look like or what would happen to us. I struggled, I clung to hope in the darkness, and I was strengthened for the season we are in now—one that requires daily sacrifice, strength, and humility. I know that our fight is worth it.

Stronger Because of the Fire

The fire I thought would destroy me was exactly what I needed for the journey we are on now. As I write this, it's been three weeks since I've seen my husband. He is sixteen hours away running a custom harvest crew. He's fighting his hardest to keep the farm going, and I am home, trying to juggle three small children and all the responsibilities we still have here. But in this season, I have the hope Paul promised I would have. I am persevering, and I am doing it with the joy and peace that come from refinement.

I know that if I hadn't felt those flames and been refined, I wouldn't be able to walk this path. I realize what a blessing it is that from the ashes God can bring so much good. Every aspect of our lives has been strengthened, but we know it isn't our strength that sees us through. In our weakness He is strong (see 2 Corinthians 12:9). So, we continue to speak the truth that is nourishment to our souls—that in the fire we are being refined. First Peter 1:6–7 says, "In all this you greatly rejoice, though now for a little while you may have had to suffer grief in all kinds of trials. These have come so that the proven genuineness of your faith—of greater worth than gold, which perishes even though refined by fire—may result in praise, glory and honor when Jesus Christ is revealed."

We're all going to walk in the fire; if not now, it will come sooner or later. The world we live in is unfair and full of hurt, and no matter how hard we try or what defense mechanisms we use, trials will come. Because we know they are part of this broken world, we know we can't choose to say "No thanks" and avoid the struggles. But we can choose how we use them.

Wherever we are, we can know that it's not for nothing. We can know that what the Enemy uses for destruction, God can use for redemption. We can know that even when our emotions try to dictate what we believe, we can hold on to the truth. Even when our world is turned upside down and nothing makes sense, Paul is still right. We can trust that if we just continue to hang on, we will come out with hope.

When we feel the intense heat of the flames bearing down on us, we know we are being held by the Refiner. As a piece of silver is purified in the refiner's fire, our impurities are being burned away by the flames. And with His eyes fixed on us, the Refiner will pull us from the fire at the exact right moment. It won't be our timing; it will be His.

The fire is hot and uncomfortable, and we could choose to let no good come from it if we harden our hearts. But if we allow the fire to refine, redeem, and restore us, then we will come out looking more like His image. We will be able to say that while the fire wasn't our first choice, it left us purified as it burned away the impurities of our hearts. Whatever our fires may be—whether financial struggles, broken marriages, sick children, the pain of loss, or anything else thrown at us—we can expect them. We can expect the pain that comes from living in a broken world, but we can also expect the comfort that comes from having a savior who walks through our pain with us.

Jesus wept with those who were hurting and grieving, and He walked with them in their pain. I hope that today if you're in the searing flames, you hold tight to the truth. I hope that even if your faith is the size of a mustard seed, you keep going. I pray that you continue putting one foot in front of the other and remember that with refinement comes redemption.

I know it doesn't feel like it, but we will be strengthened in the Refiner's fire. And if we keep clinging to Jesus, we'll come out with perseverance, character, and hope. We'll be stronger for the next fire we face. I don't believe everything happens for a reason, but I do know God can use any situation for His glory. So, when the fire feels unfair and too hot, remember that He isn't finished with you yet. Remember that whatever we have to walk through, God can redeem and restore it. Let's tuck that truth deep into our hearts. Let's keep it there safely guarded so when the fire feels too hot to bear, we can pull it out and remember the truth.

5

Gettin' Down on the Farm

Learning to Take a Marriage from Barely Surviving to Thriving

I knew I was going to marry him the second I saw him. I realize how cliché that sounds, but it's true. I also realize that teenage hormones could have played a part in that irrational thought, but I digress. I was a senior in high school, and as I pulled my silver Impala into the driveway, there in our backyard sat the most gorgeous boy I had ever seen. He leaned forward on his horse and smiled at me. His biceps stretched the sleeves of his T-shirt, and his bright blue eyes captivated me at first glance. My parents introduced me to their friends' son who had moved back to our little hometown to take over the farm after his dad passed away.

I flashed my best smile and thought about how not cute I must look after showing up from tennis practice. My sweaty hair was thrown into a messy bun that was more messy than bun, and I had one leg of my sweatpants pulled up to my knee because someone decided that was the cool way to wear your sweatpants that year. As we began to make small talk, I wondered how strong was too strong to come on with my flirting, especially with the disheveled look I was rocking.

That night we started messaging each other, and we stayed up talking well into the middle of the night. I was just a few months from graduating from high school and moving away, and Jake was a few years older than I was, firmly planted in our small town, and busy taking over the farm. I knew that realistically a relationship probably wouldn't work, but I wasn't much for listening to logic.

He made me laugh like no one else could, and I couldn't look into his gorgeous eyes without my heart racing. The smart thing to do would have been to stay just friends, but we were two young kids who didn't really care what the smart thing to do was. I fell hard and fast, and we spent the weekends driving dirt roads and listening to the country oldies station in his old beat-up Ford pickup. We were reckless and irresponsible, and we went too far too fast. We had the kind of summer you watch in the sappy chick flicks as you daydream that you're the girl on the screen.

In the middle of the pasture, we danced under the stars on the bed of his truck. An old George Strait song played over the staticky speakers as the stars illuminated our dance floor. I wanted my sappy movie to never end. I wanted to stay in that moment, soaking in the feeling of new love that turns your world upside down.

Jake taught me how to drive the old wheat truck, and I spent my first harvest tanning on the hood of the truck between loads. As summer started to wind down, I knew that the day I moved to college would probably be the end of our relationship, whatever our relationship was since we hadn't really defined it. I just wanted to enjoy every second I had with him, and as much as I begged that summer to never end, it did.

The day I moved to college, Jake helped my parents move me into my dorm room. As I watched him pull out of that parking lot in the back seat of my parents' car, I wondered what would happen next. We had both avoided the awkward conversation, but neither of us planned or really wanted a long-distance relationship. Though, if I'm honest, I wanted whatever allowed me to keep him.

Before I could even make it inside my dorm, I heard the familiar ding of my BlackBerry. A text from Jake said, "I didn't realize how much I was going to miss you." I don't think I'd ever smiled so big in my life. That text changed the entire course of my life. Every weekend one of us would make the three-and-a-half-hour drive to see the other, and every evening I would sit in my dorm room for hours, feet dangling off the edge of my bed, listening to his voice on the other end of the phone.

When I came home from college the summer after my

freshman year and Jake proposed, I was only nineteen. People told us that we should reconsider, that we were still babies and didn't stand a chance. Every time we were met with doubt, we let it roll off our backs, insisting we knew best and believing love alone would get us through whatever we might face. Oh, how naive we were.

When the Love Fades

As we were adjusting to married life—and, less than a year later, parenthood—the love didn't feel as strong. It had been pushed to the background as we tried to navigate our way. There didn't seem to be a single topic we could agree on. We put on happy faces in public and then had petty arguments the entire way home. Resentment continued to mount, while our love seemed to dwindle.

We went into marriage knowing it wouldn't always be easy. We knew marriage would require work and sacrifice, but we didn't truly grasp just how much that entailed. My sappy chick flick had ended, and I was no longer asking for a fairy tale but instead for just a little more contentment and a little less warfare. Most of our married friends shared the same stories, so it seemed normal to have these struggles, a lack of peace, and—dare I say?—even a lack of joy in our marriage.

But one day I decided I couldn't do it anymore. I couldn't keep going with this charade of a happy marriage, knowing that it felt as if we were failing miserably.

I wanted more, and I hated the feeling of resenting my husband. I wanted to go from surviving to thriving. I didn't want to be okay with a mediocre marriage any longer.

I knew exactly what I needed to do. I had known for months but had been too stubborn. I had let embarrassment, shame, and guilt keep me from what I knew I needed more than anything. I desperately needed Jesus.

I grew up in the church, was baptized in middle school, and was involved in all the church groups and youth conferences. I was raised in the faith and never had what felt like a huge come-to-Jesus moment. When I left for college, I also left behind my church attendance. I backslid in my faith, and while I still claimed to be a Christian, my evidence to back up that statement was lacking.

Jake hadn't grown up in church as I had, and he also had a lot of unresolved anger toward God for his dad's death. Faith was never really something we talked about, and it definitely was not a priority in our marriage. It was the topic we always danced around. It was off-limits.

But that day I was tired of being lukewarm and too prideful to admit I didn't have it all figured out. I knew I couldn't do it alone anymore, and I sat on the living room floor, back against the end of the couch, as I watched our baby boy playing. I couldn't keep up the act any longer, and the weight of my guilt and the heaviness of my shame threatened to strangle me. The chains were too strong for me to break, but I knew who could.

I went running full force back into the arms of Jesus. I swallowed my pride, and I stopped shoving away the Holy Spirit, who was begging me to come back. Like a dam breaking, all my emotions and hurt came flooding out. I lay on the floor and felt tears running down my face as I stared at the living room ceiling. I surrendered it all as I laid down my shame, pride, anger, resentment, and guilt.

I ran into the wild love that had never left and asked for grace and mercy and forgiveness. I asked Jesus to pick up the pieces of my shattered heart and glue them back together. I asked to just be held because I was too weak to stand on my own two feet. My fight had left me worn and weary, and I had nothing left to give.

As I ran full force into my faith, I looked back to see my husband standing still. While I was clinging to Jesus with all I had, I was alone. I was going back to church, aching that I was going without my husband. I looked around on Sunday mornings at all the husbands and wives holding hands during the sermon as I sat there next to an empty pew seat. It seemed as if the closer I grew in my walk with Jesus, the more my husband wanted nothing to do with it.

I used every strategy I could think of to convince my

husband to go to church with us. I begged and pleaded. I appealed to logic and presented historical facts to get Jesus into his heart. I came at it from every way I knew how, but nothing worked. He didn't feel the way I felt. We were still broken, and I didn't know how to fix us.

As the months passed and I prayed, studied, and let God work on my own heart, I wondered why things weren't getting better. Why wasn't God fixing my husband too? I was being more of the godly wife who showed grace and was nagging and arguing less, but things were still tense. I was holding up my end of the bargain, so why wasn't God?

The more I talked, bargained, and dug my heels in, the more Jake resisted. One day I sat at my dining room table, opened my Bible, and read the words of Peter. He said, "Wives, in the same way submit yourselves to your own husbands so that, if any of them do not believe the word, they may be won over without words by the behavior of their wives, when they see the purity and reverence of your lives" (1 Peter 3:1–2).

I sat there, reading that verse over and over and reflecting on the last months of our lives. I read that my husband should be won over by my behavior, not by my begging, explaining, and persuading. I needed to let him see the change in my own life and let God do the rest of the work. I needed to hand this battle over to God and do my part in prayer. It was my job to take responsibility for being the wife God wanted me to be, even if my husband wasn't who I thought he should be.

Right then and there, I changed the battle plan for my marriage. I began to fight in prayer *for* my husband instead of fighting *with* my husband. I prayed that it would be my actions that let him know something was truly different. I prayed that God would move in mighty ways in his heart and also in mine. Redemption and restoration were what I petitioned God for. A marriage that reflected Him, that was built on His foundation, and that radiated love, grace, humility, mercy, and forgiveness.

I wanted the joy and beauty that I knew God designed marriage to contain. I wanted to live out verses like Romans 12:10: "Be devoted to one another in love. Honor one another above yourselves." And 1 Corinthians 13:4–7: "Love is patient, love is kind. It does not envy, it does not boast, it is not proud. It does not dishonor others, it is not self-seeking, it is not easily angered, it keeps no record of wrongs. Love does not delight in evil but rejoices with the truth. It always protects, always trusts, always hopes, always perseveres." I wanted my marriage to exemplify those verses.

Little by little, I watched as God called my husband—his heart transforming from stone to flesh in his chest. I watched him soften, and I saw glimmers of hope that we could be restored. I watched as God relentlessly pursued my husband, working in His powerful, mysteriously beautiful ways.

Instead of getting up on Sunday morning and begging Jake to go to church with us, I would dress the children and myself and kiss him goodbye with a smile. I would tell him to have a good morning at the farm and that we would see him after church. I would look him in the eye and tell him I loved him while, on the inside, it took everything I had to not beg him to come with us.

I had to keep trusting that God was working in him, because I was powerless to change my husband. No matter what I said or how badly I wanted it, I wasn't the one who could elicit a change in his heart. But I did have the power to let him see Christ in me. I could let my actions reflect Christ's love.

To be quite honest with you, I hated doing this. An old adage says, "When you fight with your spouse, you can choose to be right or you can choose to be happy." For so long, my stubborn flesh wanted to be right. I would go to great lengths to prove I was right. I would prove my point and then beat a dead horse just to make sure he knew how right I was and how wrong he was.

But now if I wanted to show my husband that Jesus was real, I had to live it. I had to walk the walk. I had to truly allow God to change me and mold me. When I wanted to argue and prove my point, instead I showed grace. I showed him the mercy, forgiveness, and love that

I didn't think he deserved. Because I knew I didn't deserve those things from Jesus, but He extended them anyway because of His radical love.

Though that time in our marriage was hard and we were down in the dirt trying to figure life out, my husband was still a good man. He was a good father and a good husband even when I didn't deserve it. He treated me right. But we were two kids who had hot tempers, and I couldn't let anything slide. We were still maturing and growing; we just weren't doing it together.

After God had been slowly transforming his heart, Jake agreed to sign up for a men's conference that some friends and I had begged him to go to. In order for a person to attend this conference, both she and her spouse were strongly encouraged to sign up. The men went the first weekend and the women the next. Jake had agreed to go solely so I could attend the next weekend. When I saw him pull into the driveway after his weekend away, I opened the front door to greet him. He grabbed me in his arms, and I was embraced by a new man: A man who no longer had a heart of stone toward God. A man God had pursued and called into His love. A prodigal son who had returned home.

That was the turning point in our marriage. It was the turning point that I can take no credit for. The moment when Jesus had chipped away at Jake's heart until He broke through his doubts and barriers. We lay in bed that night and tears streamed down my face as I listened to my husband pray over me. The same husband who a year earlier wouldn't even entertain the idea of praying together.

That might sound like a fairy-tale ending and the ultimate love story, but we know that reality has a way of kicking us in the face when we think things are going well. We know that the Enemy wants nothing more than to destroy what God has deemed good. He wanted to rip Jake away from his newfound faith, and he wanted to break me.

Mending Fences

When we build fences on the farm, we have to make sure they are strong on every side. We have to regularly check them to ensure no section has been knocked down. We could have two miles of fence, but if even a few feet are broken or missing, the whole fence is useless. Any farmer or rancher will tell you that if your fence has a hole, the cattle will find it and get out.

Our marriage was a fence that had been neglected and put through storms and wear. It had so many holes that you wouldn't know where to start mending it. Weeds had grown up and become entangled in it. It felt overwhelming to take on the task of trying to mend this broken fence. At times it seemed as if maybe it would be easier to call this fence a loss and to scrap it and build a new one.

But one day at a time and one broken strand of barbed wire at a time, we began mending. We rebuilt our marriage, and the second time around, we made sure our fence was strong. We began the work of repairing and restoring our marriage, weaving in the strand of our faith and creating a fence that is not easily broken. We repeatedly failed, but we repeatedly asked for and gave forgiveness.

We gave grace when it was the last thing on our hearts; we fought our battles in prayer; we drew nearer to God and, in turn, drew nearer to each other. We brought God into every aspect of our lives. We decided we would rather be happy than be right. Hand in hand, we continued mending our brokenness, leaning on God to keep us going.

And in all God's great splendor, the day I thought I would never see came. I stepped into the cool water of the baptismal font, following our preacher. With tears of joy streaming down my face and a smile that couldn't be wiped away, I watched my husband step down into the water with us. I looked over to see our toddler leaning against the edge, watching with eyes wide.

As our preacher asked, "Do you believe that Jesus is the Son of the living God, and do you accept Him as your lord and savior?" memories and emotions overwhelmed me. Like an instant replay, I saw all the moments that had led to this one. I saw God's plan and goodness coming together in a great display of love. Together the preacher and I lowered Jake into the water until it washed over him. When we lifted him back up, we lifted up a new life. Out of that water came a new man and a new love. Out of that water came thousands of answered prayers. Out came mercy and grace and a resurrection of love.

This moment didn't bring ease or permission to take a break from our efforts. We quickly found ourselves up against mountains that seemed too large to climb. But the difference was that we didn't have to climb alone anymore. God was front and center in our lives, and He was leading the way.

We became intentional with our daily actions, and we made our relationship a top priority. We frequently failed and had to ask the other for forgiveness. We periodically slipped into our old ways and let our flesh win out. Every day we had to continue battling for our marriage through prayer and through our choices to continuously love each other in every situation.

We realized that the small actions and words had a much larger impact than we thought and that to be happy ourselves, we needed to put the other's happiness first. We sacrificed, and we did the hard, crucial work to make our marriage not just good but great. We didn't expect to make our marriage perfect, but we wanted to make it truly joyful and cherished.

We had to analyze every part of our marriage and continue to seek out what we could improve. We had to stop shoving down our emotions and start having the hard, uncomfortable conversations, including ones about our sex life. I knew I had to stop seeing sex as a chore, and I needed to get my confidence back after three pregnancies had left my body jiggly in places I didn't like.

I'll never forget the night I lay in bed and my husband wrapped his arms around me and prayed for our sex life and for amazing sex for both of us. With three small children and a mountain of priorities, most of the time sleep sounded better than sex. A talk with a good friend reminded me that God created sex in marriage to be great. He created it to keep us connected to our spouses, and sometimes we need to change how we view and prioritize it.

I began praying daily for our sex life and for the ability to see it through the lens of the gospel. And as weird as it felt to ask God for an amazing and intimate sex life with my husband, it worked. It's now something I look forward to instead of a chore I dread. It's a top priority in our marriage and is always one of the first topics I ask about when someone comes to me for marriage advice.

Momma, I understand that at the end of the day, after we have been smothered by toddlers, spit up on, and pooped on and after we have not had a single second to ourselves, getting in the mood seems like an insurmountable task. I completely get it. But can I remind you of a gentle truth? Sometimes it's exactly what we need. It takes us from being exhausted moms to being wives again. It reconnects us with our husbands and puts us back on the same page in oneness.

It's also incredibly fun to flirt with your husband. When I send Jake a flirty text, it takes me back to those days when we were dating. It gets my heart beating faster and builds the anticipation of seeing him. We should be able to have fun with our spouses like we used to when we were dating.

A great sex life is not the only way we can strengthen our marriages, but it probably makes the most impact. It encourages us to truly put our spouses first: their needs, their happiness, their feelings. It's an act of love that keeps the spark alive and constantly reminds our spouses that we are still in this. It communicates that in the middle of motherhood and adulting, we can still make choices and sacrifices to show our spouses that we care about them. This is the opposite of what the world would say, but it's the solid truth.

Time to Fight

One of the biggest ways my husband shows me he loves me is by making my coffee every morning. I try to get up early in the morning to read my Bible, but I am well known for snoozing my alarm approximately eighteen times. So, every morning when my first alarm goes off,

Jake crawls out of bed and heads to the coffeepot. He makes my coffee and then crawls back in bed, whispers "Good morning," and tells me that my coffee is ready.

He doesn't do that for me every morning because he enjoys it; he does it because he is choosing to put me first. Marriage is about all these little daily choices that add up to something big. It's about being intentional with our actions and knowing how we can put our spouses first. It's putting in the effort because it's what God calls us to do, even if our spouses aren't putting in the same effort.

If your marriage looks pretty broken right now, let me encourage you that there is hope. It's no easy task to have a good marriage, and it's even harder when only one person has his or her head in the game. Focus on you and your heart. Let God change you first. Keep pressing on and keep praying because there is hope ahead even if you can't see it. Restoration and redemption are possible through God, even if your situation seems hopeless.

Our fence looks pretty good right now, but every day Jake and I have to check for holes. We have to kill the weeds before they grow too tall, and we have to put in the time and effort to keep it in good shape. Our marriages are worth putting in the sweat equity. We don't have to settle for marriages that are merely surviving. It's possible to have marriages that thrive, but we have to put in the work.

We can choose daily to fight for our marriages, even if

we are fighting in prayer alone. We can choose grace, forgiveness, and love, even when we don't want to. And we can choose to give our husbands a smack on the rear when they get home. Every day the choices we make will determine the paths of our marriages. And if we allow God to write our stories and we trust His plan and allow Him to work in us individually, we can have marriages that make the sappy-chick-flick girl wish she were us. Lasting, joyful, beautiful relationships with roots that run deep.

6

Will the Rain Ever Come?

Learning to Lead with Faith

"In Jesus's name we pray. Amen." Jake finished his prayer, and we lifted our heads, our eyes locking. I gave a desperate smile to signal my shaken hope still hanging on by a thread. I squeezed our middle son's hand, squatted down, and placed a kiss on both boys' foreheads. Then I rose back up, lifting our baby girl back onto my hip.

I looked all around us as we stood in the middle of the field in silence. I took in the details of the scenery that surrounded me—the trees in the distance had stood the test of time, the rolling fields met the horizon, and the old barn kept watch on the hill. Slowly we walked back up to the house. The wilted wheat surrounded us. Both boys ran ahead, playing tag and shrieking with laughter, while Jake and I followed hand in hand. He gave my fingers a firm squeeze, his way of letting me know it would be okay.

A bittersweet feeling coursed through my veins. Uncertainty and fear lingered, threatening everything we knew. A heavy cloud of doubt and hesitation surrounded me, but each step across the dry soil became a step of surrender. With every move came a little more courage and fire. With every weighted footprint I could feel my faith growing and the fog dispersing.

This year was nothing new. It was yet another year of devastating droughts, record-low crop prices, and an unknown future. The talk at the local coffee shop was always grim. Men who had farmed for sixty years were wondering how they could make it one more with these circumstances. We knew we had no control of the rain, sunshine, or prices, but when those things are in your favor, how easy it is to let that slip to the back of your mind. It's when the rains don't come, the crops won't grow, and there are no options left that reality sets in.

But this year was different. We were still in the same boat as everyone else, but this time I wasn't the only one leaning on faith to get us through. I had my husband standing next to me as he held my hand and our children's hands and prayed for our faith, our farm, and our family.

I listened to this man next to me who a year earlier would have never prayed aloud. I felt the rough calluses on his hands from years of hard physical labor. I listened to the strongest man I know surrender to God. I listened to him lead our family in the presence of the Lord and pour his heart out in the middle of a parched wheat field. During that prayer, I realized that our circumstances hadn't changed but our hearts had.

In the midst of the valley we had been walking through for what seemed like ages, hit after hit knocking us to our knees, a new joy arose. I had a new song in my heart and a seed of hope that couldn't be taken. The sorrows of our circumstances couldn't trump the joy we held tight. It was the joy that came from letting go of all we held dear and simply trusting that the author of our story wouldn't fail us.

It felt like years that I had been at battle over my husband's salvation. I had put on the armor and gone to battle, believing he would *really* know Jesus. I knew our family wouldn't survive if the head of our household couldn't lead us in faith, and I had refused to let the Enemy win. So, every day I fought. Some days I thought giving up would be easier, but I had a seed of hope propelling me onward another day.

I longed for the day when I could hand over the reins and step down as the spiritual leader of our family, so fervently I battled for my husband's heart. Day after day I suited up and went to war, knowing I had God on my side fighting with me for my husband and my family.

And after the battle was won and the Enemy was defeated that day in September when my husband rose out of the water—a man after the heart of Jesus—I was tired. I had been fighting so hard, and I wanted a break. I wanted to rise out of that valley and relax on the mountaintop for a while. I wanted a break from the Enemy's relentless attacks and needed a moment just to pause. But we all know it doesn't normally work like that. Many times when we think things are starting to look up, we are knocked right back down.

Days before we prayed in the wheat field, Jake and I had sat at our dining room table and discussed our situation. "There has not been a drop of rain for months, the crops are all dying, and the cows are going to run out of grass soon," I said. "What are we supposed to do now?"

Jake looked me in the eyes and said, "I don't know, but God will provide for us. He always has." I felt tears welling in my eyes, but they weren't tears of fear, frustration, or sadness. They were a joyful response to God's faithfulness and perfect timing.

After years of praying for my husband and striving to be an example of loving like Jesus, I rejoiced when those thousands of prayers finally came to fruition. Yet there I sat just months later, questioning God's faithfulness. I had watched Him bring a prodigal son home but didn't believe He would bring the rain.

Oh, I knew He *could* bring the rain, but would He? With everything out of our control, would He come through for us again? Every time we would begin to dust ourselves off and stand up, we'd be hit with something else to knock us back down. Just when we thought we were making progress, something would come along and put us in our place.

But at our dining room table, my weary faith was held up by my husband's. I watched the transformation in his heart as he handed over our lives piece by piece. First he handed over himself, and now I watched him hand over each part of everything he held dear. He surrendered the deepest parts of his heart.

He loved his farm with everything he had in him, and so did I. There was not a single thing he would rather do than take care of the land and his animals. If that man had more money than he knew what to do with, he would still spend his days working on this farm. To most people, that doesn't sound logical, but that's the kind of love a farmer has for this way of life.

As Jake continued to grow in his faith, his prayers changed. We had both been praying for God to save the farm; really, begging God is more like it. Our prayers were soaked with desperation, fear, and a lack of trust. There was no faith evident in the way we prayed.

But on that day in the wheat field, Jake's prayer changed. "God, Your will be done with this farm. Even if I'm not supposed to be a farmer anymore. Your will." My heart dropped when I heard those words because I knew that while that was a giant step in Jake's faith and I was amazed at God's work in him, I couldn't imagine how hard it must have been for him to utter those words aloud.

"Your will" became the new prayer. In the face of desperation, we voiced our faith daily. We held each other up when we became too tired to stand on our own. Every day we prayed, "Your will." When our voices shook, our faith steadied us. We had to daily surrender what we had taken back up and tried to control.

See, the thing about faith is that it isn't easy and it isn't always our first reaction. It's a conscious choice in the face of doubt and unbelief. It's a vulnerable yet powerful surrender of our very selves. We have to continually live out our faith every day. We have to put it into action in every circumstance we face. Our mouths can profess faith, but our actions have to match up.

Philippians 4:13 is one of the most well-known and recited Bible verses. Paul said, "I can do all things through Christ who strengthens me" (NKJV). We see it printed on jerseys, painted in watercolor on beautiful canvases, tattooed on wrists, and posted anywhere else a person might need some inspiration. Like so many other people, I tucked this verse in my pocket and held on tight.

But I think a lot of times we get this verse wrong. We take it to mean we can do anything we want because we have Jesus on our side. We can win the championship game, become the best in our profession, get the promotion, save the farm, or do whatever it is we want to do. We think that this verse is our permission slip from God to do what we wish and that He will make sure it happens because we are Christians and that's our reward.

But this verse is simply Paul's declaration of contentment in his circumstances. He knew what it was like to live with plenty, and he knew what it was like to live in need (see verse 12). He knew that his contentment in his circumstances came from being strengthened by Christ. This verse was his *even if.* Even if he was in prison shackles, God was still good; his strength came from Christ alone.

I tucked that verse away to remind me of contentment, to remind me that while I would change our circumstances given the chance, I could choose to be content where we were. Because I had Jesus, I could be perfectly content and choose to have joy in the face of trials. I could turn my faith into action. I asked God to change my heart and to give me contentment despite my circumstances instead of making my circumstances comfortable enough that I could muster my own contentment.

I had to say *Even if.* Even if we lost everything we owned and had to start from scratch, God would still be good. Even if we lost our farm and were left standing in the ashes, our strength and hope in Christ would keep us going. We could still have joy in the midst of heartache. We could be content.

Paul expressed the same sentiment in 2 Corinthians

12:9–10: "He said to me, 'My grace is sufficient for you, for my power is made perfect in weakness.' Therefore I will boast all the more gladly about my weaknesses, so that Christ's power may rest on me. That is why, for Christ's sake, I delight in weaknesses, in insults, in hardships, in persecutions, in difficulties. For when I am weak, then I am strong."

Those are some powerful words, friends: "My grace is sufficient for you, for my power is made perfect in weakness." And truthfully, that can be such a hard concept to grasp. That no matter what our situations are, grace is sufficient. That whatever we're facing, no matter how painful or bleak, His grace is sufficient to see us through. When we are weak, then we are strong.

Being Christians doesn't mean God is going to swoop in and save us from pain and heartache. Surrender isn't our ticket to getting rid of our problems; it is our proclamation of faith when faith doesn't come easily. It is knowing we have joy even when happiness is in short supply. It is also making sure we don't get the two confused.

There was nothing happy about the circumstances we were walking through, just as I am sure you have faced trials that made you believe happiness was a thing of the past. Maybe you've suffered a broken marriage, infertility, the loss of a child, depression, anxiety, a disability, or a broken relationship—a situation when hope was hard to hold on to and faith seemed like an empty promise.

This is where joy comes into play. Joy is not the fleeting feeling of happiness that we chase down for a few seconds for that rush of emotion. Happiness comes from the people, events, and things around us. It slips from our grasp at a moment's notice and leaves us scrambling to get it back through whatever means we can. Happiness can quickly become the idol on which we focus, keeping it at the forefront of our lives.

But joy is where true happiness lives. It's more subtle, lingering in our hearts, reminding us to keep going. Joy is cultivated inside our hearts, rooted down deep by the hope we have in Christ. In the face of hard times, it can become battered and wilted but stays rooted as it weathers the storms and as we cling to the promises of Christ.

In the middle of that wheat field, I didn't have happiness, but I did have joy. No fear of the future, uncontrollable situations, or hard times could steal it. Romans 15:13 says, "May the God of hope fill you with all joy and peace as you trust in him, so that you may overflow with hope by the power of the Holy Spirit." And that's just what He did.

We kept our hope and we continued to trust. With every rain that narrowly missed us, we continued to hold tight to our joy. We prayed that our hearts would remain content, even in the face of drought and devastation, and that whatever the future held, we would know for certain that God already had it under control.

Weeks later, we stood on the back porch and watched the raindrops pelt the ground. For hours and hours we listened to the slow, steady rain hitting the windows of our farmhouse. A gentle, beautiful reminder of God's faithfulness in all situations. A reminder that the rain will always come. It won't come in our time and maybe not even this side of heaven. But because we have a faithful God, it will always come.

Wherever you are today and whatever you're facing, I hope you will cling to that truth. I hope you can tuck these verses in your pocket to pull out when you need that reminder. As we surrender our circumstances and we trust God to handle them in the way He knows is best, we will feel the beauty in that lasting joy that cannot be taken. Until those raindrops soak into the thirsty soil of our souls, we will pursue joy and contentment, knowing they're coming.

7

Giving God My Children

Learning to Trust

The farmer walks out into his field and crouches down. He scratches the soil, looking for a kernel of wheat. It's been days since he planted the field, and now he waits. He searches in the dirt for signs of life, to see whether the seed has germinated and is starting to grow. He looks for progress and hope, a signal that he did his job correctly. Yet he knows the result is out of his hands.

He does everything in his power to give that kernel of wheat what it needs to turn into a healthy, thriving plant that will bring a bountiful harvest. Before planting, he prepares his soil, making sure the dirt has the nutrients it will need. He waits for the temperature to be just right before sowing to give the seeds the best chance of sprouting.

He chooses the best variety of seed, and when all the conditions are right, he plants it. He parks his tractor, waits, and prays. And he has to trust. He has done everything he knows to do until this point. He has listened to his expert crop consultants, and he has poured in his time, effort, and money in hope of that seed thriving.

But in the end, it's not up to him whether that plant will grow. He does not have the authority to force new life to spring up from the soil. He has done his part, and he must trust that God will do the rest. Prayers will be sent up time and time again for God to send the rains and the sunshine and to protect this crop. These are the things he is helpless to provide, and so he trusts.

Some years the steady rains come, the conditions are near perfect, the hail stays away, and we are blessed with an abundant harvest. Other years we are desperate for a drop of rain to quench the parched ground, the seeds don't germinate, or the crops burn up from the sweltering heat. Sometimes a summer storm just days before harvest leaves an entire crop lying in the dirt with no way to be salvaged, and we are faced with acres of devastation. Regardless of what will happen, the farmer plants the seed, year after year, not knowing what is in store for it and having little control over the outcome. Yet even in the years of devastation, he knows that God is still good.

When Motherhood Comes with Fear

Not unlike the farmer and his seeds, mothers don't have control over their children's future. When the nurse laid that first baby on my chest, my world was turned upside down. Emotions and hormones surged through every cell of my body as my mind tried to process what had just happened. I remember feeling so many unexpected emotions yet not really knowing the root of them or how to sort through them as I tried to soak in the reality that we were now parents.

The joy of that moment is indescribable. If ever there were a time that a heart could physically burst from joy, that would be it. I lay in that hospital bed as we stared at this life that had just been brought into the world, and I marveled at the miracle God had created. I thought about all the details that had to come together to create this baby I now held in my arms.

I had done my part to get him here. I had taken my prenatal vitamins, exercised, eaten healthily, gone to all my checkups, and done everything I knew to do to get this baby into the world safely. But ultimately, it wasn't up to me. Thousands of things could have gone wrong that I would have had no control over, but I had to trust.

There was no reason I deserved a healthy baby when so many women don't get that chance. I wasn't so good, holy, or righteous that God would grant a healthy baby to me rather than to another woman. That's not how God works, but sometimes it can almost feel that way, can't it? We think that if we are good and do our part, then we will be dealt a good hand. And so begins the cycle of fear as a mother. Before the baby is even in our arms, we begin the game of *What if?*

Amid all those emotions in the first moments of becoming a mother, one struck me harder than the rest, even over the joy. Heart-wrenching fear hit me like a freight train. Fear that now that this child was outside my womb, I could no longer keep him safe. Now millions of forces could harm him that were even further outside my control: accidents, germs, bad people . . . so many things could go wrong.

That fear grew right along with that sweet baby. It controlled every move I made as a mother, with my sole purpose being to keep this child safe. It dictated where we went, what we did, and even how I prayed. It became a comfort that I held tight. I trusted that fear to lead me down the right path. It kept me locked in a prison of my emotions, but that prison felt like safety.

When the Fear Fails Us

I don't believe that every fear we have is unhealthy when it comes to our children. God gave us motherly instincts to help guide us, and those instincts can tell us when something is wrong. It's not the feeling itself that is the problem, but it's what we do with that fear that makes the difference.

Our children are our line in the sand with God. We tell Him that He can have control of everything else. We will follow His commands, we will go where He calls, but

He cannot be trusted with our children. And even if we say He can, do we really mean it?

Society tells us that this overwhelming fear is normal. It just comes with the territory of being a mother, and we should all get used to it. Fear makes us good moms, and it just means we love our children. But God tells us over and over throughout the Bible not to fear. He tells us to trust Him, and that includes trusting Him when it comes to our children. Isaiah 26:3 tells us, "You will keep in perfect peace those whose minds are steadfast, because they trust in you."

For the sake of authenticity, I'm here to tell you I did not trust God with my children—not even a tiny bit. There was zero chance I was going to let go of the fear that was my guiding arrow. It was all I had known since becoming a mom, and it had been working, so what reason did I have to turn over the reins and trust God with this aspect of my life?

Five years and two more children later, our middle child, Porter, got sick just before his second birthday. I am talking about not just a cold or the flu type of sick but scary sick—hospital stays, flying across the country for specialist appointments, countless lab draws, X-rays, ultrasounds, bone marrow aspirations, and one helpless, exhausted mother. The doctors told us they thought he had leukemia, then arthritis, then a heart condition. For two years we went round and round, trying to find answers, all the while being completely powerless to heal him.

My fear had led me astray. It had gripped me and become my idol, and it failed me. I had done everything in my power, and my fear was revealed as a liar. I fed my kids nutritious foods, made sure they took their vitamins and got plenty of sleep, and loved and cared for them, yet there I sat in the oncology office with my pale, limp toddler draped across my lap.

The storms had come, and I believed I had the authority to stop them. I willed them to turn their course from that once-thriving life, yet I found my efforts futile. The power I thought I held through my fear proved to be useless and deceiving when up against this storm.

Do you want to know the worst part of this story? The whole time, I had been telling God to let me handle this whole motherhood thing, yet when things went south, I blamed Him. I couldn't give Him the credit when my children were healthy and thriving, but I could sure hand over the blame when they weren't.

In the first few months of Porter's illness, I didn't realize how bad my anxiety had become. With no more tears left to cry, I was having horrible episodes of panic that left me hyperventilating. Everyone around me could see it was eating me alive, slowly consuming my soul and taking over, but it still felt normal. I still saw it as righteous and noble worry. I was simply a loving mother terrified for her child.

Do you know what God says about worry, though? He

doesn't call it righteous or noble at all. Jesus said in Matthew 6:27, "Can any one of you by worrying add a single hour to your life?" Over and over God commands us to not worry, but how can something that feels like such a natural reaction in motherhood be overcome?

As hard as it is, we have to choose. We have to choose whom we are going to listen to, and we can choose only one—God or fear. We can believe that God loves our children even more than we do and that if our worst fears come true, He is still a good God. We can put our trust in God alone, not in our efforts or emotions. Or we can choose to believe Satan's lie that tells us we should run the show and we don't need God in our motherhood. We may even let God in on some aspects, but there is no need to fully trust Him with our children and their health, safety, and futures. I would also bet most of the time we don't even realize we are holding back trust from Him.

Remember back in the second chapter when I reached my breaking point and could no longer carry the heavy burdens on my shoulders? When I lay on my floor and told God "Anything"? Well, that surrender included my children, both my exhausted efforts to keep them safe and my children's lives in general. It included Porter and his health. I quit trying to pretend I was God to my children, and I allowed God into my motherhood.

He had been waiting on my sincere surrender, and it had finally come. When my walls were broken down and

I hit the floor, surrender was left. I knew He loved my children even more than I did, and I could see I was doing more harm than good by trying to keep them protected and carrying the weight of my anxiety.

Overwhelming peace came with that surrender—and freedom to be the mother I had longed to be for so long. Not to throw all caution to the wind and become careless but to trust that I cannot control everything and that I can rest in the knowledge that God loves and cares for these children. He created them in my womb, and He knew how much I would love them.

Taking Back Motherhood

Too many mothers believe the lie that fear tells them. Too many of us have lost sacred parts of our motherhood to fear, and we can never get them back. We have done the work, put in all the effort and care, and yet still believed we are in control. We have believed we have the authority to fully control the outcome.

We can take only so much before we crack. We can hold the weight of the world on our shoulders for only so long before we break. We were not designed to carry this burden. We were not created to be the ones in control of everything. So many of us have learned to trust God with our lives . . . until it comes to our children.

God knows how much we love our children, but so does Satan. It's the perfect opportunity for him to sneak in and get a foothold while our hearts are vulnerable. He slides in and makes fear look as if it belongs, as if it comes as a package deal with the baby. Here is your precious bundle of joy, and here is a heaping side of fear that now consumes you.

But, friends, we do not have to let it be that way. We do not have to let the Enemy steal our motherhood any longer. We have the freedom in Christ to choose to entrust those precious gifts to the One who made them and loves them even more than we do. Philippians 4:6–7 says, "Do not be anxious about anything, but in every situation, by prayer and petition, with thanksgiving, present your requests to God. And the peace of God, which transcends all understanding, will guard your hearts and your minds in Christ Jesus."

I know how hard it is to let go of that fear and truly surrender what we can't control. But I also know the immense joy and freedom of not having to carry that burden any longer. Knowing I am loving and raising my children the best I can and leaving the rest to God as He guides me through motherhood is a breath of fresh air. It allows me the freedom to be the mother He has called me to be, one who isn't completely consumed by fear.

That doesn't mean that I don't worry about my children or that fear doesn't sneak in. Our instincts as mothers are usually right, and those shouldn't be ignored. But we can't let fear of the unknown future be our focus. We can't let things beyond our control decide how we parent.

We live in a fallen world with sickness and death, and things can happen that we never could have prevented. A while back when Porter was going through a really bad spell, I was talking to my preacher about the what-ifs. I wondered aloud whether losing my child would destroy my faith in God. I would like to think it could withstand that unimaginable tragedy, but I wasn't so sure.

He nodded, acknowledging my concerns, and said, "I see all the families in our church that have buried their children, and I see their faith. I see how much those tragedies have strengthened their faith in God and that in the midst of their horrible pain, they have joy in knowing that because of Jesus, they'll get to see their children again someday. They have seen how God can bring even a glimpse of goodness from their pain."

I watch friends who have lost children praise God and preach that He is still good, that He is bigger. I see them using their own scars to help heal other hurting hearts. They didn't ask to be put in that situation, and they would give absolutely anything to have their children back. But they're letting God use them to bring healing and hope to others. They're spreading the gospel, and they're not letting the Enemy destroy their faith.

When fear tries to sneak back into my heart and plant

its flag, I surrender it to God, and I think of the example those friends have been in trusting God. I hand over those fears, and I remind myself that I can't entertain those *What if?* thoughts. I choose to say *Even if* instead of *What if?* Even if the unimaginable happened, God is still good and worthy of praise.

We often joke that on our farm, we raise children, crops, and cattle. It's our silly little phrase, but it reminds me to trust. Just as my husband cannot control the outcome of the seed he plants, I cannot ultimately control the safety of my children. Both require great trust.

Even today we don't have all the answers as to why Porter was so sick or why he is not as healthy as he should be. But I still trust God with him. I still surrender my children and my control over their well-being. I refuse to pick up that fear again and allow it to steal the precious moments of my walk through motherhood.

Motherhood seems to go hand in hand with fear, but they don't have to be a package deal. Everything changes when we start saying *Even if.* Let's stand up and refuse to waste our motherhood worrying about things we have no control over. Let's love our babies well and show them Jesus. Let's show them mothers who turn to God in the face of fear. Let's trust the One who formed those babies in our wombs and reclaim our motherhood.

8

I'm Broken Too

Learning to Heal Through Vulnerability

I shut the door behind me and sank to the floor. I sat alone in my laundry room and leaned against the washing machine as I sobbed, tears streaming down my face. After weeks of holding back my emotions, trying to remain strong, keeping everything locked inside, the dam had broken. I had done exactly what needed to be done for the last several months, but I had hit my breaking point. I could no longer keep acting as if everything were fine.

The kids were taken care of, the house was running fairly smoothly, and every night the kids and I would FaceTime Jake, who was sixteen hours away. We would smile and say we missed him, and I would tell him everything was fine on the home front. I knew the stress he was under, and I didn't want to add to his worry just because I wasn't strong enough to deal with my own weaknesses. I needed to just pull it together for a few more months.

But my emotions had been building under the surface, and now there was no stopping them. Shoving them down and pretending they would go away was not working. No longer could I contain my exhaustion and loneliness. Pressing on like the strong, independent woman that society was telling me to be was killing me. So, when the dam finally broke, all my emotions came rushing out. Violent, uncontrollable sobs shook my body as I let my anguish pour out there on the floor.

I felt the weight of my brokenness, and I wrestled with my own mind. I knew the emotions I was feeling were completely authentic and overwhelmingly intense, but I also believed the lies that told me I had to suck it up. I had to shut my mouth and push through because my problems weren't big enough for my emotions to be valid.

Knowing there were people who had it much worse, who would love to have my problems instead of their own, didn't take my pain away; it just added guilt and shame to the other emotions I was trying to avoid processing. I was furious at myself that I couldn't muster the strength to get it together, that I was that weak.

When the tears finally ceased and I sat there feeling like a pathetic heap of failure, I sensed it. *No, God, not this. Please. I'll look so stupid.* I sensed the all-too-familiar tug on my heart. The one that doesn't let up when I know God is leading me into vulnerability. It's the feeling I usually try to avoid. Each time I sense this tug, I have to choose whether I will be obedient. I've learned to discern this feeling and more easily recognize when God is pressing me to share something.

The problem with that feeling isn't the discernment, though. It's following it up with obedience. It's one thing to know where God is calling me, but it's a whole other ball game to act on that knowledge and step out in faith. My instinct is to post cute pictures of my kids and say how much I love motherhood or to post a picture of my husband and tell the world how lucky I am, but who am I serving with that message? There is nothing wrong with posting those things, but if I am sharing only that facade without also sharing the down-in-the-trenches moments of life, then I am looking to serve myself and my ego instead of serving God.

When I started writing with the goal of bringing encouragement through the gospel, I ignored God's whispers to my heart several times. I had excuse after excuse as to why I couldn't be vulnerable on social media. *God, no one wants to hear that. They will think I'm a bad wife. They will think I'm a bad mother. They will think I'm a bad Christian. No one can relate to that. I'm the only one struggling with this. I don't want to show my sin to the world. I don't want to air my dirty laundry.* I would lay these excuses before God, and each time I would be met with a whisper in my heart: *But will you still obey Me?*

Over the last couple of years, it has become easier to

share the most vulnerable parts of my life with the world because I have seen the power it holds. I have had the aha moment of *Ohhh, God! That's why You wanted me to share that! I get it now!* I have seen the divine healing that has been born from vulnerability not only in my life but also in the lives of the women who have written me tons of messages from all over the world.

No longer do I want to share the curated, beautiful highlight reel on social media while I try to jump on the suitcase to get all my baggage zipped away tight and hidden from the world. I've become pretty good at showing the hard and messy parts of my life in the hope that those who read my words will feel a little less alone. I have used the *Faith, Farming, and Family* blog to extend and invite vulnerability, knowing the power it has.

And based on the number of messages I get, I've found that it has been worth it. I've read messages from women who long for their husbands to come to Christ, from ones who are lonely in motherhood, from ones who feel unseen, unheard, unloved, and unappreciated. Some messages, comments, and emails have made me laugh and rejoice, and others have brought me to my knees in tears of grief for a fellow human in pain.

I've listened to how women felt a little less alone after reading my words and how they were reminded of God's truth in the midst of their struggles. I have given God all the glory for allowing me to have a tiny role in reaching those hearts, and I've been amazed at the ways He has moved through my simple act of obedience to Him. I have seen vulnerability bring beauty time and time again.

People are often shocked when they hear I'm naturally a fairly private person. Seeing as how I've openly talked about the hardships in our marriage, financial stresses of the farm, our sex life, my struggles in motherhood, and my biggest failures and sins, their eyes normally widen when I tell them I hate being vulnerable online. I don't like stepping forward and sharing my faults, struggles, and sins with the world. It's terrifying, and it makes my armpits sweat, but it's worth it every time if it helps even one person feel a little less alone or a little more encouraged in her journey.

Even though it isn't the easiest thing for me to do, God continues to tug my heart to be vulnerable. He presses me to get my pride out of the way and let Him work. I've had to lower my shield and expose myself to the possibility of pain. I've had to step forward, slowly raise my hand, and declare that I am not okay, I am not put together, and I do not have a perfect life in the hope that someone out there will say, "Me too, but I thought I was the only one."

Throughout these pages, you have read story after story of some of my most vulnerable moments. I have shared stories I've never told before. I have poured my heart and soul into each word with the prayer that God would use this book for His glory and kingdom. I know the healing this can bring and the way God can move through these stories to touch the hearts of those reading them. I know just how powerful God is and how only He can take some of the most broken parts of our stories and make something beautiful out of them. I know He can take what we think will hurt us and use it to bring healing to us.

I've seen the wounds vulnerability can begin to heal and the mercies God brings into the midst of them. When women reach out and tell me their struggles, when they lay down their shields and risk being vulnerable, I know it's worth it. I can say, "Sister, you are not alone, and here is what God has to say about your situation and about you." This vulnerability opens the door to sharing the gospel with them because I know that my own words cannot compare.

It still makes my heart race to lay my darkest places out there for the world to see. Being vulnerable isn't just being honest with people. It goes much deeper than that. Its purpose is connection and community. It lets others know they aren't on an island alone in their struggles. Real vulnerability comes with the risk of getting hurt, but it also comes with the chance to heal.

The Strength of Vulnerability

Our natural tendency is to avoid pain. We want to run as far as we can from it and never look back. The problem with that, though, is that Jesus never promised us pain-free lives. In 2 Timothy 3:12, Paul said, "Everyone who wants to live a godly life in Christ Jesus will be persecuted." We can't outrun trials, but God has given us the beautiful gift of being able to heal and find community through vulnerability with one another.

I wonder what would have happened if Paul had ignored God's call to share his vulnerabilities. In Romans 7, Paul tells us he is frustrated that he has the desire to do good but cannot carry it out (verses 18–19). He is vulnerable in exposing his sin and shortcomings, and because of that, I can read those verses and say, "Yes! I feel you, Paul! Same here!"

What if he hadn't written those words for fear of what others would think? What if he had said, *I can't write that, God. They'll see I'm a failure.* I'm the first to admit just how much I need Jesus, and I've shared with you many times when I've failed. But there is still something frightening about laying that failure on the table for the world to see.

Or what if Paul hadn't told us about his hardships? He could have put on a brave face and thought, *I'm not going to talk about the things I've gone through because I know others have had it worse.* But because he listed the hardships he had faced, he was able to boast in the power of Christ (see 2 Corinthians 11:23–27; 12:9). He told us that his weakness was the perfect opportunity to show the strength of God's grace in his life. When we bring vulnerability to the table, God shows up with His grace every time.

I think we tend to view vulnerability as a weakness, when in reality it is a strength. It's trusting that God is going to move through our weakness to display His power. It puts God's glory on display, and it starts a chain reaction of hearts being moved. It allows us to share the story of God's glorious redemption in each of our lives.

When We Aren't Really Fine

As I sat on my laundry room floor, exhausted to the core of my bones, I picked up my phone. *Okay, God. I'll obey. Use me.* I opened my Facebook page, and I poured my heart out to thousands of strangers. I let the words flow from my fingers, praying this vulnerability would bring healing and hope to someone. Anyone.

I shared that I was struggling. I wrote how the season of life we were in was flat-out hard and I had been dancing around that fact as I tried to keep a smile on my face. Friends and family would ask how we were doing, and with tired eyes and a forced smile, I would reply, "Oh, we're fine."

Fine. That word rolled so easily off my lips but could not penetrate my heart. I was not fine.

Trying to shift my perspective only brought more shame, trying to hide my struggle only brought more exhaustion, and trying to ignore my feelings only brought more bitterness. As I wondered why God was asking me to make a fool of myself in the eyes of all my followers, I hit Publish. I cringed, knowing that while I had become good at being vulnerable, this took the cake.

Sharing this situation and these emotions I had been trying to keep locked up was deeper than I had ever gone. I had admitted the times I had failed as a mother and a wife, and I had even exposed my own struggle with the sin of gossip. But it took my breath away to admit just how much I was falling apart on the inside because I wasn't strong enough to keep marching on and being "fine."

Then the messages started rolling into my inbox. Notification after notification of comments, shares, and messages from other women. Each woman telling me she wasn't fine either. She was also tired of putting on a brave face and trying to dance around her emotions instead of just accepting that her hard situation was in fact just that—hard.

Whether it was the woman who had a miscarriage and thought she should be fine because she hadn't actually gotten to meet her baby before the baby died or the woman who was incredibly lonely because she didn't have any close friends, each one came to me, confessing her hard situation and feeling a little less alone in knowing that someone else was struggling. She'd been sitting in the same shame and guilt I had been, and she finally felt the freedom to take a breath and accept her emotions.

As I replied to those messages, reminding each woman that God's power is made perfect in our weakness, something happened. I didn't see it at first, but slowly I realized what God had done. I had shared my story in the hope of helping someone who felt desperate and alone. I wanted that person to read my words and know in the depths of her soul that she was seen and heard and that her pain mattered to God. But I began to see that God wasn't just touching the hearts of others. He had used my vulnerability to bring great healing to my own heart also. I had dragged my feet, kicking and screaming, not wanting to post my struggles, and God had taken them and redeemed them. He used those women reaching out to me to bring healing to my weary soul. I had felt alone, and those messages reminded me that I wasn't. Because I had been obedient and shown vulnerability, those women felt confident in doing the same and extended their vulnerability to me.

That is the chain reaction, friend. That is how God uses a small act of obedience to display His power. It is one of the many ways God redeems and restores brokenness. Through those messages, God shattered my chains of shame, guilt, and bitterness from believing that my pain didn't matter. He reminded me that He sees my pain and that His grace is sufficient for me. Most of all, He reminded me that His power is made perfect in weakness.

As you read these words, I bet there is something that keeps popping into your mind—something you've felt as if you have needed to say or do. But you've let the fear of vulnerability hold you back. What if you didn't let it hold you captive any longer?

The next time you have the opportunity to allow God to bring healing through your vulnerability, whether for you or for someone else, I hope you'll take it. I pray you will have the courage to step out in obedience and allow Him to use that vulnerability for something beautiful. Let God take those deepest parts of your heart, those things you think can bring only pain, and allow Him to bring them into the light, where you may find redemption, beauty, and healing.

Vulnerability is a beautiful gift God has given us; we just have to shift our focus. We have to see it for what it is, and we have to step out, knowing that God will use it for healing in the hearts of those around us and in the hearts in our very own chests. Today I hope you will start that chain reaction and watch how God moves in your beautiful and brave act of obedience.

9

The Bountiful Harvest

Learning to Feel Both Grief and Gratitude

She hugged my neck and told me she had been praying for us. "I don't understand how you have been so thankful through all that you guys have been through," she said. It wasn't the first time I had been told that. Thousands of people were praying for Porter as we battled to find out what was making him so sick, and the easiest way to keep everyone updated was through my Facebook page.

After each doctor appointment or new development, I would post an update about our situation. People were invested in us and wanted to know how he was doing. At the end of every update, I would say something I was thankful for and would express that God was still so good—whether the news was good or bad. I wasn't trying to show everyone what a good Christian I was or how strong my faith stood in the midst of a trial. I saw it as an opportunity to share the gospel and show that my strength came from God alone.

So many people were following our story, some of whom weren't believers in Christ. I knew the truth that God was good no matter what we faced, and I knew I could be thankful in the situation, even if I wasn't thankful *for* the situation. I wanted to share that message with everyone reading our updates. I wanted to make it clear that I knew God was on our side, even if the situation wasn't one we asked for or liked.

Being thankful in the midst of our situation didn't mean it wasn't painful. It didn't mean I wasn't consumed with worries and fears that my worst nightmare might come true. It didn't mean I didn't go over all the what-ifs and allow the darkest thoughts to enter my mind. It just meant I knew that God was bigger. And I knew that even if God chose not to heal Porter, He was still a good God.

I know in the depths of my soul that God can redeem any situation. I know that only He can take the very things we think have crushed us beyond repair and bring something beautiful out of them. Our pain isn't taken away or forgotten, but it doesn't go to waste. He takes that pain and breathes beautiful life into it. He picks up the pieces of our shattered souls and forms them into something only He can make. Beauty and redemption come out of our broken stories.

The Farmer's Redemption Story

The story I'm about to tell you is not my story, but it is an amazing illustration of God's powerful, redeeming grace. It is my husband's journey to redemption from brokenness, and it started before we even met.

The summer heat sweltered as Jake walked across the stage in his cap and gown and accepted his high school diploma. The rest of his class went to graduation parties, but Jake went home and packed his bags. Within an hour of graduating, he was headed to Texas, and he was on top of the world. Two of his biggest dreams in life were to go on a harvest crew across the country and to be a cowboy on a large ranch. His first dream was coming true, and life was working out exactly as he had planned.

It was the summer of 2008, and he had the opportunity to go harvest wheat with a friend who owned a custom operation. He had loved being in a combine since he was a toddler, and he was no longer the eager little boy in a dusty ball cap sitting on his dad's lap and wanting to steer. Now he was the one in the operator's seat. His dad and grandpa had spent the last eighteen years showing him the ropes of the farm, letting him learn hands on, right alongside them.

A few days into harvest, he stood in the parking lot of the motel, filling his water jug with ice before starting the day. "Jake, can you come to my room for a minute? I need to talk to you," his friend said.

Jake followed his friend to the room. "I don't know the right way to tell you this, and I'm so sorry that I have to be the one to tell you, but your dad was in a car accident last night and didn't make it."

Just like that, Jake's dream turned into a nightmare. The way he had pictured his life shattered to the ground before him. A boy full of hope, joy, and a love of life instantly turned into a man filled with earth-shattering heartbreak. Life as he knew it was gone and could never be restored.

I've never experienced that kind of pain and shock, and I can't imagine what it felt like or how deep the pain went. I think of how shattered Jake's family must have felt as they tried to decipher the next move, picked out which boots to bury his dad in, and searched for the perfect song to play at his funeral that would capture his life. I can't imagine the sorrow and agony Jake experienced as he stepped into the role of farm owner and tried to figure out the details of an operation that was now his responsibility.

I can tell you that when "Amarillo Sky" by Jason Aldean comes on the radio, I see my husband catch his breath. I see the signs of his dad, Donnie, all over this farm. Every day I open our mailbox that was made by his dad, I see the metal Kansas State Powercat mascot that hangs off it and I smile that he was a huge K-State fan also. I grin whenever people tell me that Porter reminds them of Donnie and that I should be worried because that is a whole lot of orneriness to try to handle. I love that while I never got to meet him, I can look back at pictures from my parents' wedding and see Donnie standing with my dad as a groomsman.

But I can't fully know my husband's hurt. I can try to understand, but I can't truly know the intense weight of the grief or the responsibility his father's death placed on him. I have no idea the emotions he must have felt as harvest started at home and they hauled in his dad's last crop less than a week after his funeral. I do know, though, that for many years, Jake was angry at God. He blamed God for taking his dad away, believing Satan's lie that God was the one to point the finger at, that God wanted to bring him pain.

A few years ago, I felt such a weird mix of emotions as Jake brought to me a realization I hadn't thought of before. "Caitlin, if my dad hadn't passed away, we probably wouldn't be married or even know each other. We wouldn't have our family, and I probably wouldn't really know Jesus like I do now."

That's an odd feeling, knowing that something tragic happening is what started the chain of events that caused your life to work out a certain way. Jake is not thankful he lost his dad, nor should he be. It still hurts, and he still grieves daily. He hates that our children don't know their other grandpa, and he misses him with everything he has. What Jake is thankful for, though, is that God didn't just leave him in that grief alone. He is thankful for a God who can bring something beautiful out of pain.

Expect the Suffering

We know that it's not God who brings the brokenness (see John 10:10). He is not the author of evil in this world, and though He protects us from so many things, we will each have to walk through the dark valleys. They're just part of the world we live in. The hope comes from the fact that He doesn't leave us there and doesn't ask us to walk through them alone. Jesus walks through that hurt and brokenness with us.

No one asks for grief to come his way. We don't long for days when we face sorrow, doubt, sadness, pain, and heartbreak. Yet throughout Scripture, God reminds us to expect them. Peter tells us in 1 Peter 4:12–13, "Dear friends, do not be surprised at the fiery ordeal that has come on you to test you, as though something strange were happening to you. But rejoice inasmuch as you participate in the sufferings of Christ, so that you may be overjoyed when his glory is revealed."

I know that for most people, including Christians, those words are a hard pill to swallow. We want life to be fair, pain-free, and wrapped in a pretty bow. God allows pain to come our way, but He isn't the one who brings it. He isn't plotting the ways He can hurt us; He is orchestrating how He will use our pain to draw us closer to Him. How He will redeem it and how He will show His glory through it. Romans 8:28 says, "We know that in all things God works for the good of those who love him, who have been called according to his purpose."

Our trials look different, but they all have something in common. No matter how big they are, God is able to redeem them. They aren't too hopeless, too painful, or too hard for Him to bring beauty from the ashes, even when our hurt wants us to believe otherwise.

In John 16, Jesus told His disciples that He was going to be leaving them and they were about to face a whole lot of trials. He told them that things were going to be hard, but He reminded them that their grief was only temporary, while His peace is never ending. In verse 33, He said, "I have told you these things, so that in me you may have peace. In this world you will have trouble. But take heart! I have overcome the world."

Before he really knew Jesus, Jake thought death had the final say. Now he knows that isn't the case. Jesus conquered death, and our sufferings cannot compare to the joy that is coming (see Romans 8:18). If you're in the middle of suffering, that might not bring much salve to your wounds. But take heart, friend. Romans 8:35–39 says,

> Who shall separate us from the love of Christ? Shall trouble or hardship or persecution or famine or nakedness or danger or sword? As it is written:
>
> "For your sake we face death all day long;
> we are considered as sheep to be slaughtered."
>
> No, in all these things we are more than conquerors through him who loved us. For I am convinced that neither death nor life, neither angels nor demons, neither the present nor the future, nor any powers, neither height nor depth, nor anything else in all creation, will be able to separate us from the love of God that is in Christ Jesus our Lord.

God is not in the business of making orphans, widows, barren wombs, car wrecks, abuse, divorce, poverty, injustice, or whatever other heartbreak this world brings. He is "a father to the fatherless, a defender of widows. . . . God sets the lonely in families, he leads out the prisoners with singing" (Psalm 68:5–6). He is our refuge and strength, our comfort and hope, our restorer and redeemer.

The Kernels Must Be Broken

During planting on the farm, I love to watch the wheat kernels pour into the planter as we prepare to start the new season. The tractor pulls the planter across the ground, placing each seed just beneath the soil. I watch the kernels run through my fingers, trying to fathom how from these tiny kernels, there soon will come a field that, God willing, will yield a bountiful harvest.

What is the first thing that has to happen to those kernels before they can produce a crop? They must be broken. Their shells must be cracked open before anything beautiful can be made. New life starts to spring forth from that brokenness. Slowly, ever so slowly, those plants are nourished and continue to grow. They become stronger and stronger, breaking through the surface of the earth—out of the darkness and into the light.

We have to trust that out of the brokenness, God will bring new life and growth in us. That is why we can be thankful. Our pastor explained this once by breaking down Matthew 16:24. We can be thankful that because we love Jesus and want to fulfill His will (follow Him) more than we care about our own lives (denying ourselves), He will take those bad things (our crosses) and make them good because He cares for us. We might not know just how He is going to do that, but we can have faith that He will.

This is why Jake can feel both grief and gratitude, and it's why I can feel both uncertainty and hope. Earlier, I referred to the first half of John 10:10, which says Satan "comes only to steal and kill and destroy." You know the best part of that verse? The second half, where Jesus said,

"I have come that they may have life, and have it to the full."

It's so easy to get hung up on our pain and put our focus on what has been destroyed in our lives or taken from us. It feels natural to keep our eyes on the things God has allowed to happen to us. But God's kindness is displayed not only in our pain but also in every moment of every day, through the bad and the good. Romans 2:4 says, "Do you show contempt for the riches of his kindness, forbearance and patience, not realizing that God's kindness is intended to lead you to repentance?"

I recently asked Jake what the turning point was for him that enabled him to stop blaming God for the pain in his life. All the pain he had been wrestling with hadn't taught him that Satan was doing bad things and God was doing good; rather, it was the kindness of God that our pastor shared with him a few years ago that changed Jake's heart. God brought good from that pain, but He did it with His kindness and mercy. He could have left Jake alone in his grief and brought nothing good from it. He didn't owe Jake anything. But because He is a kind and good God, He allowed goodness to come from Jake's pain.

I see how God brings redemption from our pain, but I also see His goodness on display every day. I see His goodness in the newborn calf as it stands on wobbly legs for the first time. I see it in the sun that peeks over the barn every morning as the sunrise paints the sky. I see it in friends and family who step in to lend a hand and paint my living room. I see it in a church that helps teach our children about Jesus, in Finley's curly hair that bounces when she runs and laughs, in Grady's crooked and genuine smile, and in Porter's ornery grin that puts a smile on everyone's face.

God has used situations both good and bad to draw me to Him and to lead me to repentance. I can't put God in a box and believe there is a situation He can't use. I don't have to know how He will use each situation; I can just be thankful that He will. "Give thanks in all circumstances; for this is God's will for you in Christ Jesus" (1 Thessalonians 5:18).

10

Back to the Simple Life

Learning That Living More Simply Invites Greater Joy

I had waited for this day for years. In my dreaming, planning, and anticipation, one thing always worked its way to the front of my mind. For years we had prayed to be able to buy the farmhouse, and that dream was coming to fruition before our very eyes. Every detail was falling into place, and after years of waiting, the answer to our prayer was finally yes. I scrolled through Pinterest as I contemplated decorating ideas and color schemes. I gathered paint samples, and I dreamed of the sound of my children's feet running across those worn hardwood floors.

Finally we would be living on the same farmstead where Jake's grandpa had been born and raised, where his grandma had rung the old bell on the back porch that signaled it was time to come in for dinner, and where Jake had spread his dad's ashes down by the barn. Our children would be the fifth generation of Hendersons to call this old farmhouse home.

I couldn't wait to be able to walk out my back door and take a few steps to the shop to surprise Jake with an iced tea instead of having to drive the fifteen miles one way, as I had been doing for the last six years. I dreamed of the day I could look out my dining room windows and watch our cattle grazing down in the pasture. My heart longed to be at the farm for so many reasons, but I looked forward to one thing the most: the front porch.

I thought of what it would be like to sit on my farmhouse front porch, coffee in hand and Bible in my lap as I watched the sun peek over the horizon. I imagined the talks with God I would have in those early-morning hours. I envisioned the scene in my head of our kids shrieking with laughter as they played tag on a summer evening. I pictured Jake next to me, holding my hand and just being present in that moment with nowhere else to be.

I imagined so many moments on that porch. I couldn't contain my excitement when friends asked me how I felt about moving to the farm. I let them in on my dreams of my porch, and I was met with looks of confusion. It probably seemed silly to be so joyful about something so simple. But their perplexity about my joy didn't bother me because I knew just how precious those moments would be.

I remember spending hours sitting on the porch of my

childhood home, surrounded by siblings, parents, and grandparents. Those joyful memories of catching fireflies, blowing bubbles, and sitting on Grandma's lap are so clear in my mind. I knew the memories that could be made on a front porch, memories that last long after some of those people are gone.

The front porch represented a peace that so many of us strive to savor. In a world that says to go faster and that pushes us to do more and be better, our souls long for rest. That front porch represented stepping away from the ever-growing obligations, demands, and schedules and getting back to the simple beauty life offers.

Of course, I was excited for more space and a bigger bathroom, but I had learned to be content without those things, and they weren't my greatest focus. I've learned a lesson over the last few years that has changed my life and my perspective: the simple things in life have the power to bring us the most joy. The moments that are unscripted turn out to be some of our fondest memories.

Leaving Room for Life

Busyness isn't a competition, and *busy* should not be a title we wear proudly. When we fill our schedules to the max, we don't leave room for life to happen naturally. We don't leave room for the quiet moments when we hear God speak. We jump to the next tasks on our to-do lists, and our lists never end. We measure our worth by how many tasks we can accomplish, and we compare ourselves with the people next to us as we exhaust ourselves trying to keep up. We push the things that truly matter to the back burner as we allow other activities to take up our time.

We believe the lie that if our kids aren't in every activity offered, then we are depriving them of the experiences they need to be shaped into functioning adults. We feel the pressure to do and be everything—all at the same time. We are pulled in every direction as we try to live up to the moms who seem to have this all figured out. We see the facade they put on and take it as truth, and they're looking at us doing the same thing.

We struggle with feelings of inadequacy as we wonder why we are the only ones floundering through motherhood and life, just trying to keep our heads above water. We are all so busy struggling to keep up with one another that we are left exhausted and wondering how we got to this place. We aren't sitting down to eat supper as a family because we have too many practices, recitals, board meetings, conference calls, and games that we're pulled between. Our lives are so jam-packed with activities that we barely see our own families, let alone spend quality time together.

I don't think we mean for this to happen, but it's a process that slowly consumes our entire lives. As our oldest child started getting to the age where activities are offered left and right, it just seemed like the natural thing to do. His friends were participating in the same activities, and it felt as if saying no made me a worse mom.

Every paper sent home announcing a new sport or group was promptly filled out and returned. We signed him up for soccer, the county fair, piano lessons, flag football, and any other opportunity that came our way. We filled our schedules with all the activities and ran from one place to the next all week to fulfill our obligations. Our five-year-old's schedule had just as many tasks as ours, and society was saying it was all for the greater good of his future.

My tipping point came when I had to choose between keeping our family together for the summer and letting Grady stay in his summer activities. His favorite activity was showing his calf at the county fair. The year prior, he and his calf, Sugar, had won reserve grand champion, and Grady couldn't wait to show another calf the next year.

But the next year also happened to be the year that Jake would be taking a crew harvesting for even longer. He was going to be gone for at least six months, and if we wanted to keep our family together as much as possible, it meant we couldn't commit to letting Grady show a calf or do summer sports. As I weighed our options and tried to decide whether simplifying our family's schedule in order to spend more quality time together would outweigh the benefits of the activities we were already involved in, I had no idea how this decision would change our lives.

There was no doubt that showing his calf was an amazing experience for Grady. Activities like this help shape our kids' character. This is true about sports, music lessons, or any other club or organization. So many options are available for kids to gain experience, exposure to new things, and skills, but at what cost? At what point do the scales tip and the gain is no longer worth the cost? At what point do we draw the line and say "Enough"?

These choices don't apply just to our children. They apply to us first. We draw the line for our families of when enough is enough, and over time our priorities shift without our even realizing it. We don't make time for lunch with a friend because we are too busy. We can't read another bedtime story because we have to return work emails. We can't sit on the front porch and enjoy the sunset because we have yet another activity that's filling our calendar.

I felt like I was failing because the busyness wasn't working for us. It was slowly sucking the life out of our family, and I had to wrestle with feelings of guilt and inadequacy that I couldn't do it all. I felt like I was doing a disservice to our child by pulling him out of these activities, like it was wrong of me to hold him back from these things, even though I was doing it to keep our family together.

I talk to so many other moms who feel like they're failing for the same reason. I'm not telling you to pull your kids out of every activity and never leave your house. I'm just telling you that it's okay to not do every activity offered, Momma. In this world that keeps telling us to do more and be more, it's okay to slow down and say no sometimes.

Running Our Own Race

Busyness so easily becomes a weight around our ankles that keeps us from truly enjoying our lives. It quickly crosses the threshold from productive to distracting and exhausting. Our focus is pulled away from our mission as we're sucked into time-consuming activities that leave us drained and weary.

The author of Hebrews lays out our mission clearly: "Since we are surrounded by such a great cloud of witnesses, let us throw off everything that hinders and the sin that so easily entangles. And let us run with perseverance the race marked out for us, fixing our eyes on Jesus, the pioneer and perfecter of faith" (12:1–2). Jesus is our example of how we are to run our race—not our neighbor's race, not the race of the person who seems to have it together. We are to run no one else's race but ours.

If I'm being honest with you, I was dreading that summer. My fear of missing out was overwhelming at times. As I scrolled through Facebook and saw all the other kids getting their calves ready for the fair, Satan would try to sneak in. He would whisper the lie that my children were missing out. I felt guilty, thinking I wasn't doing enough. I was lacking action in motherhood, and that meant failure. I was selfish because I couldn't keep up and was choosing simplicity for our family.

The thing I've learned about Satan and his lies is that though they can be unbelievably convincing, I have the choice to believe them or not. And so do you. We can believe those lies that tell us we need to run faster and look in the lane next to us to see what that person is doing, or we can do what the author of Hebrews told us to do—keep our eyes fixed on Jesus as we run our race.

As we prioritize what deserves to go on our schedules and what gets our attention and time, we can keep our eyes on the finish line. Will this obligation or activity be worth it, or will it tip our scales? Will it leave us exhausted and overwhelmed? We can unlock those weights around our ankles that try to slow us down and steal our focus from what's important. We can keep persevering as we stick to our race.

I sat in the combine that summer and saw the pure joy on the faces of my children. There we sat, speechless, five people crammed into the cab of a combine, marveling at the view in front of us. On the bank of the Missouri River in Mobridge, South Dakota, all my guilt faded. There was no longer a shadow of a doubt that we had made the right decision.

I sat at the top of that hill, surrounded by incredible beauty that God had created, and was so elated I had put my foot down and refused to sacrifice our summer. I was so thankful I didn't miss out on some of the best moments our family has ever had as we spent our days crammed inside a combine together and traveling the country as a family.

Do you know what happens when you are forced to sit in a small space with your family for several hours at a time? Fighting, spilling drinks, having to stop to pee a hundred times, getting a million crumbs on the floor, and someone crying because someone else looked at her funny. But something else happens in those sacred moments of togetherness.

Conversations are had that are deep, meaningful, and full of lessons. I connected with my children's hearts and souls in a way I hadn't before then because we had been too busy. I had heart-to-hearts with my husband as I sat in the buddy seat with a squirming toddler on my lap. We laughed and dreamed with each other for hours on end, and we reconnected with authentic hearts bared.

I realized I had been so busy treading water that I never got to be still. I never stopped and took a breath because I was always trying to keep up with society's expectations of motherhood. I was so busy trying to make my kids' childhood great that I was missing out on what was happening in front of my very eyes. I was working so hard to give my children the childhood I thought they needed that I wasn't giving them time to actually enjoy it.

Back to the Good Stuff

When we refuse to sacrifice our time for the sake of busyness or of keeping up with the person next to us, we can get back to the good stuff. We can enjoy the rewards that come from instilling these values in our children. We can get back to the simple joys that we would otherwise miss out on as we go through motherhood and life. We forget the abundant beauty that's hidden in the simplest moments. We forget that oftentimes it is these moments that end up meaning the most to us.

We can't see what's right in front of our faces if we are constantly looking ahead to what's next on our calendars. Our priorities shift, and we lose sight of the beauty in life. We stress about the board we agreed to be on, the cookies we have to bake for the bake sale, and the other commitments we have to juggle, and we no longer have time for what really matters.

Will I still let our children do sports, clubs, and other activities? Absolutely. But what I won't allow is for those things to become our priority and steal our time and family. I won't let our schedule be so overloaded that we can't breathe. I won't sacrifice our family's valuable time together for the sake of trying to live up to other moms.

I will also still volunteer in church, bake cookies, and help out with kindergarten art class. After all, while we have great freedom in deciding what to put on our schedules, we are still called to have servants' hearts. Galatians 5:13 says, "You, my brothers and sisters, were called to be free. But do not use your freedom to indulge the flesh; rather, serve one another humbly in love."

As I go through life, I want to be able to look back and know that my children were taught the important lessons and skills they needed for their adult lives, even if the way they learned them looked a little different from the experience of most kids. I want to know that we loved our neighbors and served others well and that we valued our time around our dinner table and refused to sacrifice it every night.

When I am old and gray, I want to sit on my front porch and remember the way we sat on the couch, surrounded by our children, with nowhere else to be. The times we took in the raw beauty of life's moments and actually savored them. I want to remember the way we sat at our coffee table and played board games and drank hot chocolate. I don't want to remember that we were too busy to have a picnic in the living room or that our schedules were so full that we didn't have time to play tag in the yard and watch the sun set.

The times when we have found the most joy have been the moments that weren't structured or planned down to the minute. To sit around a campfire and watch the joy on your children's faces as they are covered in s'mores is unforgettable. Those are the moments I want to remember. I no longer want to sacrifice the great so I can have the good.

Friend, I don't want you to miss out on these moments. I don't want you to look back and not have the memories of sunsets, s'mores, and campfires. And while I don't believe we can ever find the perfect balance, can I just encourage you today to evaluate whether you could give up good in exchange for great?

Making It to the Porch

I remember the first morning after we moved to the farm. I had gotten up at five and shuffled to the coffeepot. While I waited for my coffee to brew, I looked around at the boxes strewn about the kitchen. I cringed as the creak of the back door threatened to give away my escape. I felt the cool concrete under my bare feet with each step I took.

I made my way down the sidewalk and around to the front porch. I grinned as I sat in my chair, curling into a ball and resting my mug on my knees. As I sat there sipping my coffee, I couldn't contain my smile. I cried tears of thankfulness that this moment was as perfect as I had imagined. I watched the first rays of light break through the darkness. I soaked in the quiet and savored every minute of the long-awaited moment.

I was reminded that it's in the quiet moments that we are able to hear God the loudest. When we silence the noise and distractions and clear our minds, we can expect Him to show up and infiltrate our hearts. We can pause and remember what it feels like to just be intentionally present. We can choose to live more simply and invite greater joy as we run our race.

11
City Meets Rural
Learning That Not Everyone Thinks Like You Do

I shoveled chips and salsa into my mouth as I watched the conversation unfolding in front of me. I sat at a table with four other women, three of whom were not involved in agriculture. Their eyes lit up as I listened to my friend Terryn answer all their questions about our farming and ranching way of life. I would chime in between my bites of Mexican food, offering my point of view from our farm.

We sat at the table for what seemed like hours as we talked about our lives and how they differed, letting them in on what our days looked like. They asked question after question, wanting to hear about how we live and stating how vastly different our lives looked from theirs. We talked about everything from what we feed our cattle to how we involve our children on the farm and ranch to their disbelief that we live over an hour from a Target or Starbucks.

I've thought a lot about that conversation since it happened almost a year ago. It was in stark contrast to what I see so often online, where it seems people don't make the time or effort to see another's point of view. I see dissension as I scroll through social media, and it's deeply discouraging. It seems as though we have forgotten how to communicate with one another. We are so desperate for people to know our side of the story and to hear where we are coming from that we forget to listen to their side. We have stopped hearing people out.

I see people spending their time arguing from behind their computer screens and missing out on the productive conversations that really matter. It seems as though we have forgotten that someone thinking differently from us doesn't always have to be a bad thing. I see people directing hateful, degrading comments at others for simply stating their opinion, oftentimes on subjects that aren't even that important. Watching this happen over and over, day after day, is enough to bring anyone down, and ultimately, it isn't even productive.

But when I reflect on that conversation at the table, I know there is such value in communicating with people who don't think like us. No one on this earth is going to think exactly like we do, but it seems we've forgotten that it's okay to be different. We can find friendships and make connections with people who are polar opposites of us. And even if we encounter people who take different stands than we do, we still have the choice to be kind.

One of my biggest encouragers is a Jewish woman from New York. I've never met her in person, but through the wonder of the internet, we've been able to build a marvelous friendship. Even though we have very different views on nearly every subject, she is always there to support and uplift me. She doesn't try to change my beliefs, and I don't try to change hers. I frequently find messages from her in my inbox, telling me to have a good day or that she loves me or just checking in to make sure I'm doing okay. She shares my words relentlessly, and she is one of the most genuine women I know. We're aware of the other's beliefs, but we still come together and choose to encourage each other despite our differences.

God created each one of us beautifully unique. We are all different yet all made in His image. Each one of us. First Peter 4:10–11 says, "Each of you should use whatever gift you have received to serve others, as faithful stewards of God's grace in its various forms. If anyone speaks, they should do so as one who speaks the very words of God. If anyone serves, they should do so with the strength God provides, so that in all things God may be praised through Jesus Christ. To him be the glory and the power for ever and ever. Amen." God's desire is that we would know Him, that we would be saved through Jesus's death and resurrection, and that we would use the different gifts and talents He has given us to bring Him glory. But because we live in a world where we have free will, that is not always the case. So, what are we supposed to do when we encounter those who don't think like we do?

We listen.

When we are talking to people who have different beliefs, morals, standards, parenting methods, or anything else, we don't have to cut them off and shove our ideas down their throats. We can have conversations with those who don't think like us, and we can find common ground. We can see them as people that God created and loves, and we can meet them right where they are in that moment. We can listen to their stories and empathize with them to try to understand where they're coming from and why.

When I started the *Faith, Farming, and Family* blog, I set out to tell the story of our farm and life. As you now know, coming into farm life was not an easy adjustment for me. I didn't gracefully adapt to my new way of living, and I learned so many of my lessons the hard way. I was like a new baby calf trying to get its legs under it. Just when it thinks it can stand on its own, it topples over and has to try again.

Listen to the Whisper

One day I was scrolling through a farmers' wives Facebook group, and I kept seeing the same sentiments over and over. The markets were crashing, times were getting hard for almost everyone, people were selling their farms, and it just felt dark. So many posts radiated hurt and desperation as these women tried to adjust to this way of life or were just over the struggles of it altogether. I read post after post from wives who were lonely, frustrated, resentful, and tired. We were all so tired.

For a while during that season, I quit writing. I didn't want to talk about what was going on because it felt embarrassing and shameful to be going through such a dark time. I didn't want to pretend everything was hunky-dory while so many families were in the same boat as we were. But to admit our struggles was too scary. I wasn't ready to be that vulnerable and raw, so I went silent.

I continued reading the posts as these women shouted desperate cries for help, offered advice, and expressed comradery. And as I prayed, I felt like God was nudging me. Like He was saying, *Stop telling them about you, and start telling them about Me.* My breath caught in my throat. After all, who was I to preach to people? I was a hypocrite, a failure, and a desperate sinner in need of Jesus. I felt too flawed to be giving anyone encouragement or advice. But I listened to that whisper in my heart.

I started writing again, but I changed *how* I wrote. I still told the stories from my life, but I emphasized how Jesus was there in the middle of them. That, yes, the markets were crashing but that God is still faithful. That, yes, we were going to have to shake up our family to diversify and go custom harvesting but that God still provides. That on the days I couldn't hold it all together, His grace was sufficient. I had the promise of Isaiah 40:31:

> Those who hope in the LORD
> will renew their strength.
> They will soar on wings like eagles;
> they will run and not grow weary,
> they will walk and not be faint.

I was vulnerable and honest, always trying to find the lesson in the story and point it back to Jesus. I knew that clinging to our faith was what was getting us through those uncertain and scary times, and I needed other people to know they could have that same hope in the midst of trouble. I opened my heart, and I let people inside our real world rather than the polished, filtered one that looked so pretty and neat.

As I did that, something incredible happened. Message after message started rolling into my inbox from women who so desperately needed the hope that only Christ can offer. Women who were down to their last shred of strength were finding it was not their strength they needed to lean on when things got hard. I couldn't fix their problems, but I could point them to Jesus for comfort and hope.

I also noticed that as I started to become more vulnerable and open, focusing on the goodness of Christ instead of the goodness of me, more people showed up on my page. More people read my words to be encouraged and to be pointed to the truth. They wanted to hear about how Jesus walks through our story with us, even on the farm.

The most unexpected part of all this was the number of messages coming in from people who had very little in common with me. I read messages that said, "I don't think I have ever even met a farmer, but I love following your page and your encouragement that you give me." I was a little shocked that someone who had nothing to do with farming would want to hear our stories. I mean, yes, I was bringing a lesson out of those stories, but they still were from the farm perspective.

Then I got a message from a stranger across the country that completely shook me: "I don't even believe in God, but I love to hear your stories, and I always still get something out of them." I read that message and then picked my jaw up off the floor. I wondered why someone who didn't believe in God would continue to read posts that didn't shy away from sharing the gospel. It completely blew my mind.

Then came the light bulb moment. It's okay that not

everyone thinks like I do. For so long I thought I could write only to other farm wives who had the same convictions, standards, and morals that I had. And I applied this thinking not only to my writing but also to the people I spent my time with, the people I chose to follow on social media, and the people I spoke to at the grocery store.

I felt judgmental and dirty as I realized I had closed myself off to people who thought differently than I did. I thought about how I had failed to obey the call to go and make disciples since the only people I really associated with were just like me. I was not living out God's command to love those around me if I was drawing lines to divide who I thought did and didn't deserve love.

If Jesus had associated only with the people who were just like Him, then His time on earth would have been pretty lonely. Not only His acquaintances but also His closest friends were chock full of failures and shortcomings. They were human beings with temptations, pettiness, jealousy, pride, and other problems that got in the way of their being like Jesus. They had theological arguments, and oftentimes Jesus had to set them straight about the truth. But He did it.

Jesus hung out with the outcasts, and He loved those who thought differently than He did. He longed for them to know His heart, and He listened to their stories. He didn't pick and choose whom He came to die for but instead offered salvation to all.

In John 17, we see Jesus praying for His disciples on the night He was arrested. In verses 15–16, He said, "My prayer is not that you take them out of the world but that you protect them from the evil one. They are not of the world, even as I am not of it." So many times I hear other Christians say that we are to be in the world but not of it. And yes, it's true that we are not to be of the world but that we are to be set apart.

But I believe we need to put more emphasis on the "in the world" part. We are not called to just be wandering around in the world while making sure we are still set apart. We are sent into the world. We are called to move our feet, to be on a mission to show Jesus to the world, not just to those who think like we do but especially to those who don't.

When we get to the deep roots of what can bring us together, we can connect with those who don't think like we do. We are all humans who have wants and needs, plans and hopes, and a deep longing to be seen and loved. When we cut off the superficial layer that separates us and pushes us apart, we can see how much we are all alike.

When we take the time to listen to people's stories, to try to understand them as individuals, we can do our job as Christians better. We will see each person not as a project that needs fixing but as simply another person who needs Jesus just like we do. We can lay our judgments aside and hear others out. We can't just shove everything we know and believe at them and then wash our hands while saying, "Job well done. I shared the gospel." That doesn't work.

That's not to say we should be afraid of sharing the truth of the gospel. We should boldly proclaim the power it has and the ways it's changed our lives. We should overflow with the desire to tell others about who Jesus is, but we should do so with our hearts intent on those people knowing Jesus. We should not include judgment because we think they aren't living up to our standards and need fixing. The fixing isn't our job.

Before we look down on the drug addict, the unwed mother, the girl who sleeps around, or whomever else we look at and think, *Oh, she needs Jesus,* remember that so do we. All the people we cross paths with have circumstances that have led them to where they are the moment we meet them. They have struggles like us, trials like us, pain like us, and sorrow like us. They have bad hair days, children who won't always listen, and disappointments—just like us.

They don't need us to shut them out because their sins look different from ours. They need us to stand beside them and meet them right where they are right now. We can show up and say we're broken too. We mess up, fall on our faces, and can't seem to get our lives together either.

Thankfully, God equips us to live out the mission we have been called to as Christians. He convicts our hearts by the truth of His Word and the Holy Spirit, and He guides us back to the path when we get off track. Jesus is our example of how to love people. All people.

The good thing about lines is that they can be erased. We can't change yesterday, but we can choose what we do today. We can be the people who come alongside our neighbors, longing to fulfill the call to love like Christ, and we can lean down beside them and erase the lines we've drawn.

12
Their Success Isn't My Failure
Learning to Be an Encourager

I slid the cake pan into the oven and dusted my flour-covered hands on my apron, looking like a modern-day June Cleaver. I walked to the sink to begin scrubbing the dishes and making lunch. I watched the birds hopping around on the ground outside my kitchen window, looking for a snack of their own. It was a beautiful fall day, and my heart was full.

For the past several years in Kansas, it seemed as if we hadn't gotten much of a fall. It went straight from summer to winter, with very few of those perfect-weather days. But this day was beautiful. The sun shone brightly, the slightest breeze was blowing, and it was just warm enough that you didn't need a jacket. When those beautiful days show their faces, I get ecstatic.

I had opened the windows to let in the fresh air and done a quick clean of the house, and, as always, I felt a desire to bake something. Every time we have a beautiful fall day, I get the urge to bake. Days like that fill my cup and remind me of the simple beauty in life that is right in front of me. It reminds me to be thankful for the small things, to slow down, enjoy my day, and breathe in the fresh air.

As I placed the last mixing bowl in the drying rack, my phone rang. "Honey, could you run outside real quick and help me back up the combine to the header trailer?" my husband asked. Jake hadn't been home from harvest very long, and he was trying to get all the equipment cleaned up and stored in the sheds before winter.

The headers that attach to the front of the combine can be taken off and put on a trailer so they can be transported more easily. Jake just needed me to stand by the trailer and tell him how far back to come and which direction to go to make sure the hitches lined up.

I ran outside to the driveway, where the trailer was parked, and I held up my hand to motion to Jake to keep backing up. I pointed to the right with my thumb, trying to get the hitch in the perfect spot. "Okay!" I yelled while making the stop signal with my hand. I reached over and put the pin through the hitch, attaching the combine to the trailer.

As Jake climbed off the combine, I saw him laughing. "What's so funny?" I asked. He grinned as he pointed to my outfit. Ladies, you know the look your husband gives you when you wear that certain dress or flash that certain smile, the one that says he's really digging you? Well, for my husband, it's my apron that does him in. "You forgot to take your apron off."

I looked down and realized I had, in fact, forgotten to take my apron off. That explained the flirty grin on his face. I laughed with him and told him that if ten years ago someone told me that one day I would forget to take off my apron before hooking up a combine to a trailer, I would have fainted.

I put my hands on my hips, and I smiled a big, joyous grin that came from deep within. Jake snapped a picture as I stood in front of the combine, proudly wearing the hand-quilted apron given to me as a wedding present. That apron was my favorite, and I loved wearing it. The grease stains reminded me of the times I had tried to cook for my family in those first years and miserably failed. That apron reminded me of the memories made in our little farmhouse kitchen when I placed it on our oldest as he learned to help cook. I remember the way it dragged the ground and how he squealed with excitement when he cracked his first egg without getting shell in the bowl. It reminded me of all the hours I spent wearing it as I learned to shift my perspective from having to cook for my family to loving to cook for my family.

That night I posted the picture Jake had taken on my Facebook page. I said that God had made me a farmer's wife, that I never would have chosen this life for myself and never would have imagined this is where I would end up but that God knew what He was doing and I was so thankful. I said that I finally realized that what I was doing in these mundane, ordinary days was important work.

I realized that my role matters. Some days I do nothing but cook, clean, and take care of needy, tiny humans. Other days I run a combine for fifteen hours and get covered in wheat dust and grease. It doesn't matter exactly what my day looks like, but it does matter that I am where God has called me. And that means the work I am doing is important.

Then I reminded the people seeing that photo of me in my apron that their roles were important also. That whoever was reading that post mattered and that even if they were feeling trapped inside their homes with children or working jobs they didn't love or trying to juggle a million things at once, their roles were important; they were each seen by God.

I wanted those who read that post to know that I saw them and I understood that sometimes it feels as if we are unimportant unless we are doing something extravagant. That we don't see how valuable we are to the people around us and that God uses even the ordinary days for great purpose.

The picture of me standing in my apron in front of the

combine was my plea to the wife and mother who felt unseen, unheard, and maybe even unloved to remember that she mattered and so did her days. I prayed that whether she spent her days in an office, her home, or both, she wouldn't forget her value and what God says about her.

It took only a few minutes after hitting the Publish button for the comments and shares to start rolling in on my thread. Comment after comment echoed my sentiments, and women threw up the praise-hands emoji left and right. They said, "Thank you for this reminder" and "This is exactly what I needed tonight." They felt seen, and they were reminded of what they had forgotten.

It also didn't take long for the comments that weren't as kind to start rolling in. Women told me that I should be embarrassed, saying that I was too much wife and not enough farmer and that real women spend their time not in the kitchen but out on the farm right alongside their husbands. They told me that *farmer's wife* was a dirty saying and that I should be ashamed.

I've been doing this writing thing long enough to know there will always be people who disagree with me, and that's okay. People normally don't disagree in a respectful or kind way. They take my effort to encourage other women and use that vulnerability to rip me to shreds. Normally I can let those responses roll off my back. My skin has become thicker over the years, and I'm able to move on and focus on the comments from the women who needed to hear my words of encouragement and were touched by them.

But without even realizing it, I was taking the negative responses on this post to heart. The comments telling me I wasn't enough of one thing and was too much of the other made their way into my thoughts. I wondered whether these women were right about me and what I should do differently to be more like them. If they could boldly share such strong opinions about such a simple post, then maybe they were onto something.

I realize that to some I may look like an old-fashioned wife. I don't mind cleaning and cooking (most of the time). I love to make our house a home and to whip up a fresh cobbler for company. Honestly, it just brings me joy. I've learned that I shouldn't have to apologize for that, and you shouldn't have to apologize if you hate those things. Both are okay.

But I also love being able to hop into a piece of farm machinery and help my husband out for the day. I love to get my hands dirty, and my husband loves it when I come with him and am able to lend a hand.

This is what works for our family, and it's where God has called me to be in this season of life. He has called me to love and serve my family well and, in turn, serve Him well. In Matthew 20:28, Jesus said, "The Son of Man did not come to be served, but to serve, and to give his life as a ransom for many." If Jesus came to serve, then so did I, because my ultimate goal in life is to continuously look and love more like Jesus.

As I gave up headspace, thinking through the comments that were telling me I was doing life wrong, it allowed comparison to sneak into my heart. I began comparing my days with the days of the women who were writing these comments. I viewed us side by side, comparing our roles as wives and mothers on our farms.

I scrolled through the comments, playing the comparison game with each one. *She works on their farm full time. I'm not strong enough for that,* I thought. *She makes every meal for her family from scratch. I wish I did that.* With each thought, I compared my role with someone else's and came to the conclusion that I didn't measure up.

I had gone from being content and joyous to feeling frustrated and doubtful about my efforts. That's what comparison does to us. It comes in and tells us to look at a glimpse of someone else's life and see how we don't measure up. It starts a snowball effect, and as the snowball rolls down the mountain, it takes with it our contentment and joy. It clouds our thoughts and prevents us from clearly seeing the importance of our purpose or role.

Living Out Your Purpose

Whether or not you feel like it in this season of life, God created you for a specific purpose. When He formed you in your mother's womb, He had a plan for you (see Psalm 139:13–16). When we take our focus off letting God use us for that purpose and turn our focus to someone else, we cannot live out our own callings. Paul talked about this in Galatians 6:4–5: "Each one should test their own actions. Then they can take pride in themselves alone, without comparing themselves to someone else, for each one should carry their own load."

I don't want to spend my life trying to live out someone else's purpose, and I don't think you do either. Theodore Roosevelt is believed to have said that "comparison is the thief of joy." He was right. How much joy can we have if we are putting our efforts into striving to be like someone else?

I've been a people pleaser my entire life, so the only reason I can tell you this is because I had to put my thoughts into action. I had to stop caring about whether I was living up to others' expectations of who they thought I should be and focus instead on whether I was living up to who God wanted me to be during each season. I was not created to fit into someone else's mold, and neither were you.

When we stop comparing ourselves with the mom on Instagram who seems to have it all together (even if we know she really doesn't, because none of us do), we can turn our faces back to what God is asking us to do. We find our contentment and joy in knowing that God has a purpose for each of us and that it isn't going to look exactly like anyone else's.

And when we regain that contentment and joy in knowing we were created for a purpose, something very beautiful can happen. We can show genuine kindness and encouragement to those in the lane next to us who are striving to live out their purpose also. We can be their cheerleaders, encouraging them to keep pressing on in whatever it is they were made to do.

It doesn't matter whether they are stay-at-home moms who feel led to go back to work or working moms who feel called to leave their careers to stay home. It doesn't matter if their lives don't look like ours or if their goals and dreams are polar opposites of ours. It doesn't matter if they live on farms in rural America or in the heart of New York City. The only thing that matters is that we are focused on being who God wants us to be and that we are encouraging those around us to be who God wants them to be wherever they are at that moment.

Hebrews 10:24–25 says, "Let us consider how we may spur one another on toward love and good deeds, not giving up meeting together, as some are in the habit of doing, but encouraging one another." We cannot live out these verses if we are in the trap of comparison. We cannot genuinely spur one another on if we are overtaken with jealousy that has resulted from comparison.

Other people's success does not equal our failure. Read

that again if you need to, friend, because it's that important. Other people's success has absolutely nothing to do with us. It should have no bearing on what we do in our lives. If the lives of others have no impact on our own, why, then, is it so easy for us to look at others' success and immediately feel envy? Or if not envy, at least a palpable lack of joy for them?

It seems as if we are all in a race to get to the top, frantic because we believe there is only so much room up there. So, when we see others appearing to do better than we are, we view them as competition. Our first reaction sometimes is not to spur them on in love and encouragement but to compare their lives with ours and chalk ours up as failure.

Getting Rid of Jealousy

God slowly shows me piece by piece what my purpose is and how He wants to use me to bring Him glory each day. I know this season of life I am in is important, even though it can be monotonous.

We get to choose to trust that God made us with a unique and specific purpose and that it's a continuous process to live out that purpose. I can choose to believe that my purpose doesn't look like yours, and I can encourage you to keep pressing on toward your goals. I can urge you to remember that comparison has no place in your life and that you can choose to not fall into that trap.

When you feel jealousy creeping in, instead of allowing it to simmer in your heart, flip it upside down and reach out to that person. Something changes in our hearts when we encourage those around us. At first it might feel forced or awkward, but trust me on this. If I see another writer making great strides and that ping of jealousy comes up, I send her a message immediately. I tell her that I see the great things she is doing and that I'm proud of her. It's not a lie either. It's a deliberate heart change, because when I stop allowing jealousy to grow roots, I can pluck it up, throw it out, and truly be happy for her. I can lift her up and encourage her to be the person God has created her to be. Then I can focus better on who *I* am called to be.

I want you to live out your purpose and bask in what God has in store for you. You can start by throwing that checklist out the window. Take that piece of paper in your mind—the one that has all the ways you think you don't measure up and all the ways you believe someone else is better than you—and crumple it up. Throw it in the trash and don't allow it to get you off course for another second. Put on your metaphorical apron and show the world the joyous grin that comes from knowing you are exactly where God has called you to be.

13
Not Everyone's Cup of Tea
Learning That Not Everyone Will Like You

I was in third grade, standing on the playground at recess, surrounded by the popular girls. It was the first time they had let me stand in their circle, and I was dying to be accepted by them. I wanted to be welcomed into their group and be called their friend, and I finally had my chance.

They went around the circle, each girl saying her favorite color. The leader of the pack stated that her favorite color was orange, and all the girls quickly agreed what a good color it was. All eyes turned to me as they waited for me to state my favorite color. Such a simple task yet a moment that would be cemented in my memory and would shape my behavior in the future.

My favorite color was purple, but none of the other girls had said that color; surely if I declared that my favorite color was different from theirs, I would not be accepted into their group. I quickly decided I *couldn't* be different. I was sure of it. This was my one chance to show them I belonged, so I couldn't blow the opportunity. Without hesitation, I declared that my favorite color was also orange, and what a coincidence that we had the same favorite color! It must be fate.

That was the first moment I distinctly remember feeling as if I needed to fit in to be accepted. It was the first time I remember trying to change who I was in order to be liked. It was the first time I believed I was not good enough in the eyes of my peers. I decided I needed to run with the crowd and try my hardest to not stick out. If I could like the things they liked and do the things they did, then they would recognize that I was one of them and would truly accept me. And then I would be able to find true friendship.

As it would turn out, no matter how hard I tried to fit in with that group of girls, it wasn't enough. I wasn't invited back to the circle, and being teased and ignored made it ring loud and clear that I was not wanted. Nothing I had tried to change about myself had made them want to be my friends.

Those feelings of rejection evolved into my believing I wasn't enough. I thought I was so flawed to my core that as a grade-school girl it was already deeply ingrained in my heart that I did not belong. I let the opinions of my peers define who I was and the level of my worthiness.

I kept this mentality as I grew, constantly trying to change who I was in order to be accepted by my peers. How I talked, what I wore, the way I walked—everything I did was a calculated effort to mirror those around me in the hope of being accepted. My deepest longing was to be liked for who I was, when really I had no idea who I was. My identity was buried in my insecurity, and the root of my people-pleasing lay in the fear of failure and rejection.

I spent so much of my life exhausting myself in attempts to be liked by everyone. I constantly sat on the fence, never truly taking a stand for anything, because I knew that would mean having to disagree with someone. I avoided conflict at all costs yet thrived on the drama of those around me. I loved when people would tell me gossip, because that gossip felt like acceptance. They were taking the time to let me in on a juicy secret, and I would eat it up.

My lack of self-worth and confidence followed me into adulthood. As a new mom, I found myself trying to make friends using the same old tactics. The same longing to be liked and accepted followed me everywhere I went, weaving itself into my conversations and interactions.

I had spent so many years trying to fit in and be liked by everyone that I no longer had a clue who I was. I was more worried about what the world thought about me than what God thought about me. My self-confidence and self-worth crumbled into nothing. I was in a state of despair while trying to find my footing in life.

I believe we all have a need to feel as if we belong. We all have a longing to be truly seen, heard, and understood. We have this empty space embedded in our souls that we continuously try to fill, and when nothing fills that hole and we come up short, we become defeated and hopeless. We place our self-worth in things that were never meant to determine our value and worthiness. We find our worthiness in the opinions of others, the numbers on the scale, the friendships we make, the cars we drive, the houses we live in, the money in our bank accounts. We let these things tell us how valuable we are and dictate how we view ourselves.

One of the things I love so much about God is the way He can take our hurts and brokenness and breathe life into them. He can mold even the parts of us that make us say, "Well, this is just how I am," and He can allow us to see the truth through the lens of the gospel. He can help us surrender the beliefs we have held for years. We are able to see that the tendencies and thoughts that have run so deep through us for the majority of our lives are not strong enough to withstand the truth of what God says about us.

Unclench Your Fists

I would love to tell you there was some big, defining moment where I boldly proclaimed who I was in Christ, throwing off the need to be liked and approved by everyone, embracing who God made me to be. I wish there were a single moment when it all came crashing down and I turned around and never looked back at those insecurities and doubts. I wish I could tell you I no longer struggle with needing to be liked by everyone and I never slip back into finding my worth in the opinions of others.

Those would be lies, though. I didn't have a major turning point or a breakthrough moment that set me on the path of freedom from those chains that held me all those years. What I did have were little moments when I felt the Holy Spirit beckoning me into the truth. He used Bible verses that imprinted on my heart the truth of who God made me to be and how He sees me and friends who weren't afraid to speak truth to me, even if it wasn't what I wanted to hear.

When we are so focused on trying to be liked by everyone around us, we don't have the time, energy, or focus to hear what God is saying about us. We push to the back burner the things He is calling us to do or say because we don't want to make waves. We come up with excuse after excuse as to why we cannot be used by God because our insecurity tells us we can't make an impact, even through God.

Because I feared being rejected and being seen as a failure in the eyes of others, I lacked the faith and trust to step out in obedience to God and be the person I was made to be. My quirks and personality—all the little details that made me unique—I had hidden away for as long as possible in the hope of not being exposed as different. I had spent so many years thinking that who God made me was more a burden than a gift and telling Him I was unwilling and unable to be of any use to Him.

At this point, I had been writing on and off for three years but never going too deep. Once again my fear of failure and rejection held me back from truly stepping into what God was calling me to do. I lacked faith that writing was really where God was calling me, and I wasn't willing to put myself out there in such a vulnerable way.

Thankfully, God doesn't give up on us. I couldn't ignore the pull in my heart to trust that God wanted to use me as a tool to bring Him glory. I knew if I would just be obedient, I could trust that He wouldn't fail me, but I continued to offer excuse after excuse.

My knees hit the cold wood floor. In my fists I clenched all my hopes, dreams, doubts, fears, insecurities, and control. I held close the fear of rejection and failure that had shaped so much of my life. I held them so tightly, afraid to let them out of my grasp and to experience the consequences of being obedient. I was hesitant to unclench my fists and hand them over, not knowing what that would mean.

Finally, I opened my fists and handed it all over. Fear and rejection had nothing on the power of God's love. I told Him I would be obedient in whatever it was He was calling me to do, but I asked Him to help me know what that looked like. I had relied on myself for too long, and I needed clarity as to what exactly I was supposed to be doing.

The next evening I sat in the Suburban on the edge of the wheat field. The kids and I had loaded up our lasagna and headed to the field to feed the crew. We caught them right as they were getting ready to head to the next field, so I pulled in behind them and turned on my flashers to help them move. The only option to get to the next field was to take the highway, which we hate to do. But sometimes it's the only choice.

As I sat in the field after moving, I quickly wrote a Facebook post about following the combines down the road and asking for grace from people as we attempt to get the crop harvested. I wanted to let people know that farmers realize we are slowing others down but we're doing our best and we're sorry. I hit Publish and tossed my phone in the console. I visited with the crew for a few minutes after everyone ate supper, and then I loaded up the kids to head home.

I got the kids settled inside and sat down for a minute before starting on the mountain of dishes in the sink. I gasped when I pulled up my notifications. My post was going viral. My friends and family started texting me in disbelief and sending me screenshots of how quickly the number of shares was rising. I thought about how just a day earlier I had surrendered my writing to God and asked Him for clarity.

I sat on cloud nine as I forgot about my fears and insecurities that had held me back for so long. My request for clarity had been answered loud and clear. I was in awe at the way God had been so gracious to me, the way He had made His presence so tangible less than twenty-four hours after I unclenched my fists and surrendered.

I didn't sit on that cloud for long, though. The more shares the post got, the more comments rolled in saying vile and hurtful things about my post, me, farmers, and even my family. I was appalled at the language some people used, especially to someone they had never met who had never done anything to them. Dozens of people took the time to comment solely with the intent of telling me how much they didn't like me.

These hurtful commenters didn't know me or my story. They didn't know my heart or my intent, but based on only a couple of paragraphs, they made up their minds about me. It was cemented in their heads that I wasn't good enough for them, just like on the playground that day. I had taken the step out in obedience and shown a sliver of who I was, and that was already enough to elicit the backlash. Strangers on the internet were deciding who I was and what I was worth.

A day earlier, those messages might have made me retreat. I would have recoiled from the pain of not being able to please everyone and having to reconcile the fact that people did not like me. I would have spent hours responding to comments, being ridiculously kind and trying to show these people who didn't even know me why they were wrong about me. I would have thought that if I could just set the record straight, they'd realize they'd judged me too quickly.

I wasn't going to do that now that I had given my writing to God. As I read each comment from someone with malicious intentions, I prayed, *God, remind me who You say I am.* He had already made clear to me where He was leading, so now the choice rested on me. I could go through those comments and let them determine my worth, playing them over and over in my head, feeling the pang of rejection. Or I could accept that those people didn't like me and that I didn't need them to approve.

Their words still came with a sting, but I acknowledged it and moved on, refusing to lend space in my mind or heart to those comments. I know that because Jesus died on the cross for me, I am made new, I am chosen, and I am valuable and precious to God. That, friend, is where we should seek our worth. Not in what people say but in what God says.

This, sweet friend, is what God says about you: He created you in His image (see Genesis 1:27). You are "fearfully and wonderfully made" (Psalm 139:14). He has crowned you "with glory and honor" (8:5). Where there is sin, grace runs deeper (see Romans 5:20). You are "God's handiwork, created in Christ Jesus to do good works" (Ephesians 2:10). You who are in Christ are a new creation. The old has gone, and the new has come (see 2 Corinthians 5:17).

What the world has to say about you probably rings in your ears constantly, just as it does in mine. Every day social media, magazines, and television tell us who, what, and how we should be. They beg for our attention, luring us away from the truth of who we are in Christ. Today I pray that you will shut out that noise. I pray that you will unclench your fists and let go of your fear of rejection and failure. And today I pray that you will fiercely and wildly believe exactly what God says about you.

14

Kick Off Your Boots and Stay Awhile

Learning the Importance of Hospitality

Unworthy, unqualified, and *embarrassed.* Those were the words that went hand in hand with *hospitality* for me. Those were the words that described how I felt when the command to have a servant's heart tugged on my heart-strings. And my feelings snowballed into overwhelming anxiety at the mere thought of inviting a friend over for coffee or hosting Thanksgiving for our family.

In our creaky old farmhouse with its sloped floors, abundant paneling from eras past, and a bathroom tiled in a faded baby blue, I felt torn. I longed to have an open, welcoming home where people knew they could come and find fellowship and communion. I wanted the place that said, *I'm so glad you're here.* I wanted the home that was inviting and warm for every person who crossed its threshold. But how could I possibly offer those qualities to our guests when our home was much less than show worthy?

I saw magazines showcasing beautiful homes, with their ten-foot tables splayed with place settings and glamorous centerpieces. How much easier it must be to extend that offer when every detail seems perfect and well thought out. How much easier it must be to focus on fellowship when you aren't worried about what your guests will think about your outdated wallpaper. I thought about how naturally hospitality must come for people with homes like that, and I envied them.

It wasn't that I didn't love having people in my home. It was that I didn't like having people in my *house.* That's because I believed hospitality meant coordinating napkins, beautiful platters, and fine china. Today it seems as if hospitality is a display of what we have, as we invite our guests to share in it. Society has us believe that it is a spotless home, intricate decorations, and Pinterest-worthy themes. It becomes easy to focus on the act of hosting more than the act of hospitality.

It seems as though everywhere we turn, the focus is making sure people love our homes, our decorating skills, or our cooking rather than making sure the people inside our walls feel loved. We can easily believe the lie that if our homes aren't perfect in every way, then we are unqualified to extend an invitation. We leave it up to the person with the bigger kitchen or better-decorated home, and we count ourselves out of the equation.

At that conference I mentioned earlier, I met a girl named Brynn. She was hilarious and genuine and also felt out of place in a group of women who had never before met in person. We stood in the corner and asked the simple questions that one asks as they try to gauge another person. We laughed and cried and laughed some more. It didn't take long at all for us to become great friends.

A couple of months after that conference, she sent me a message saying that on their way home from a work trip, she and her family would be passing through Kansas. She was going to find a hotel close to me so we could meet up for coffee and a playdate. Now, I believe we all have those moments when we know without a shadow of a doubt that God is asking us to do something. The tug is so strong that we just can't ignore it. This was absolutely one of those moments.

As I read her message, I knew I was supposed to invite her and her family into our home. I knew I was supposed to extend my arms and show true hospitality—not with a perfect home but with an authentic heart. Two months prior, we had moved from a rental house to the hundred-year-old farmhouse, and with the house still in chaos, I opened the door to authentic hospitality.

This woman whom I had met in person just one time was going to be staying in our home, along with her husband and children whom I had never met. Maybe it sounds crazy, but I wasn't worried. She was one of my best friends. We talked every day, and she was a person I knew I could count on. She might have lived halfway across the country, but that was just a minor inconvenience in our friendship.

While I knew I was supposed to extend this invitation, my heart wrestled with that truth. I knew that what they needed was a kind friend, a good meal, and a place to be refreshed in hope. But I kept grappling with insecurities about the details. I kept retreating to the feelings of unworthiness because of imperfection.

I truly did find joy in the little preparations. I fluffed the pillows and placed fresh-cut flowers in an old mason jar on the night table. I made sure the towels, fresh out of the dryer, were folded neatly on the bathroom counter. I planned each meal and did the grocery shopping and meal prep. I scrubbed the toilets and picked up the toys, making sure everything was as tidy as could be. I found joy in knowing I was doing what I had been called to do. But I also did those preparations in hope that they would override my imperfect home. I still had my priorities out of order.

Putting the Details Above the Purpose

The Bible talks about how Martha and her siblings would host Jesus and the disciples. It talks about how close their family was to Jesus and how much He loved them (see Luke 10:38–39; John 11:5). Martha would slave away in the kitchen, making sure every detail was perfect. She did the cooking and cleaning, and she wanted her home to be welcoming. She longed to be a good hostess. She wanted her home to be the one that Jesus and His disciples could come to and relax in after a long day of teaching.

There is nothing wrong with striving to have a welcoming home and finding joy in the details. Besides, someone does have to do the cooking and cleaning, right? But where Martha—and I—failed was putting the details above the purpose. We focused on the minor details while overlooking the big picture.

You see, while Martha was slaving away in the kitchen, her sister, Mary, was at the feet of Jesus. Martha was worried about supper, and Mary was worried about hearing the words of Jesus. And maybe we can relate to why Martha was so irritated. We would be annoyed that the entire workload fell on us and that while we were making sure the details were perfect, everyone else was enjoying fellowship. Wouldn't we want to not have to worry about the details and just be able to feast on the words and presence of Christ?

Letting her frustration lead the way, Martha told Jesus to make Mary help her. She didn't ask Jesus for His advice or opinion; she told God what to do. Jesus brought her back to the truth that those little details aren't the most important thing. Striving to be a good hostess should never be more important than striving to show true hospitality. "Martha, Martha, . . . you are worried and upset about many things, but few things are needed—or indeed only one. Mary has chosen what is better, and it will not be taken away from her" (Luke 10:41–42).

There is nothing wrong with a good home-cooked meal and beautiful, thoughtful touches. It's okay to find joy in centerpieces and place mats. It's even okay to have a stunning home decorated intricately according to the season. But what hospitality really boils down to is the conversation that happens around a meal. It is the grace that is extended, the wounds that are healed, and the community that draws us closer to being Christlike.

A Kansas Welcome

As luck would have it, the day Brynn and her family arrived, our air-conditioning went out. What else could say *Welcome to our home* like the heat and humidity of a Kansas summer? I offered to pay for them to stay at a hotel, but Brynn, being one of the sweetest people in the world, would have none of it. She was the most gracious guest, pretending she wasn't about to sweat half to death.

We got up the next morning, poured our coffee, and sat on the couch as we watched the kids play on the rug.

We laughed and cried, and we leaned on each other for help with things we were struggling with. We sat on that couch all morning, never even getting out of our pajamas. We bared our hearts to each other, and we talked as if we had been best friends for years. In those few hours, we discussed nearly every topic under the sun, and we begged time to slow down.

We got in one last hug before I waved goodbye and watched the dust follow them down our dirt road. I stepped back inside, glanced at the dirty dishes in the sink, and was overwhelmed with joy. My shame and embarrassment because of my less-than-perfect house faded into the background, and right then and there, I promised myself I would never again let those feelings stop me from showing hospitality. I had just learned not only the meaning of hospitality but also the importance and impact of it.

On my living room couch, with toys scattered over the floor, yesterday's messy bun hanging from the side of my head, and smeared mascara on my eyes, I finally understood why we are called to be hospitable. I realized that Brynn didn't care about the outdated tile; she cared about the way I welcomed her in. She cared that I authentically wanted her in my home and that I opened my arms to her family. She cared that what genuinely mattered to me was her presence. My insecurities about not having a perfect home couldn't begin to touch the joy brought by the conversations between two broken souls just trying to draw closer to Jesus.

Today Brynn is one of my dearest friends, and I think a big part of that is because of those hours we spent on the couch with our vulnerable hearts laid before us. That invitation not only strengthened our friendship, but it strengthened me as well. It revealed to me the importance of serving others. It opened my eyes to the bond that can form while giggling and crying over cups of coffee. It showed me the value that can come from conversations around the dinner table with people you barely know.

The fellowship, the laughter, the community, and the healing that happen is why we are called to show hospitality. Jesus didn't care about the fancy dishes or the little details. He cared about the teaching and discipleship. He knew it was the words shared that would make the most impact. He knew that while Martha was just trying to be the best hostess she could be, she was getting it backward.

I've kept my promise to myself since then. I've opened my home without hesitation because I know that the bathroom that isn't remodeled and the rickety kitchen cabinets don't determine the conversations around my table. I can share the gospel in our living room despite the carpet that needs replacing. I can give encouragement with toys scattered on the floor. I can share a meal with someone even though I need to finish repainting the walls. And as much as I would love Joanna Gaines to come have a cup of coffee as we discuss decorating plans, I can be content where I am.

The Example of Jesus

All through Jesus's ministry, He was immersed in hospitality. He taught and fellowshipped at dinners that lingered into the night. He ate with sinners, outcasts, Pharisees, and disciples because around the dinner table, people felt an extension of radical love. There was such an inviting feeling that people were drawn into His fellowship.

You can flip through the Gospels, and it won't take you long to find a story of Jesus sharing a meal with someone or feeding a crowd. It's great to have a conversation with someone, but something special happens when you gather over a meal. Jesus knew that, and we are shown that example time and time again through the Gospels.

Jesus didn't ask us to show hospitality so our friends could revel in our beautiful homes. He asked us to extend hospitality to abundantly give grace and love and to follow the example He showed us through His time on earth. He knew that our neighbor who is struggling would need a warm meal and a listening ear. He knew that the woman down the street who is fighting loneliness would need a shoulder to lean on. He knew that sitting at a table with others opens doors to conversations that are meaningful and hopeful. It opens doors to showing people Jesus and the hope of the gospel.

Maybe it isn't your home that brings you insecurity. Maybe you struggle with the food and worry that your meal won't be elegant enough, won't taste good, or will look as if you're trying too hard. I can promise you from being on the receiving end of hospitality, the food isn't what matters. Make your go-to dish, no matter how simple or boring you think it is, make the meal a potluck, or even order some pizzas. Your guests aren't going to remember the food; they're going to remember how you made them feel.

If you've been hesitant about extending hospitality because you don't feel worthy, remember the words of Jesus to Martha and remember the words of Romans 12:13: "Share with the Lord's people who are in need. Practice hospitality."

Remember the root of hospitality and the depth of its purpose. Consider the lives you could touch, the souls you could encourage, and the hearts you could refresh if you followed the example of Christ and used the gifts God has given you. Think about the opportunity to make an impact at your own dining room table just by offering a servant's heart over a warm meal.

I'm not telling you that you need to have the wayward gathered around your table every night as you preach the gospel. If you are, that's great, but I'm asking you to look at your focus and see where God is calling you to be hospitable. I'm asking both of us to take a look at our hearts and really analyze whether it's Mary or Martha whose tendencies we lean toward.

Are we opening our homes in hope of being the light of Jesus that a person lost in the dark will see and turn to for refuge? Or are we opening our doors only after we have the perfect meal, the perfect house, and perfectly behaving children? If we continue to strive for perfection before we obey the command to extend hospitality, we will never get there. And even if we were able to fake it for an evening and fool our guests into believing we have it all together, aren't we missing the point?

If we can't be real as followers of Christ, then how can we expect to minister to and find communion with those who are struggling? If we are striving to be like Christ, we have to be relatable and empathetic. How can we encourage our brothers and sisters in Christ if they buy into the lie that they must be doing something wrong because their lives aren't as tidy as ours appear?

The apostle Peter wrote to the church about this, saying, "Above all, love each other deeply, because love covers over a multitude of sins. Offer hospitality to one another without grumbling. Each of you should use whatever gift you have received to serve others, as faithful stewards of God's grace in its various forms" (1 Peter 4:8–10). Peter reminds us that we each have gifts and that those gifts should be used for serving others, even in our messy, real, raw lives where we don't have it all together.

I almost didn't include this chapter because it has been such a short time since I had this shift of heart. Just because I'm okay with people coming into our home and gathering around our table doesn't mean I'm good at extending the invitation. To be completely honest with you, I'm still pretty awful at it. It feels hypocritical to be telling you why hospitality is so important. I get so busy with the daily activities of my life that the thought of asking whom I could minister to today doesn't cross my mind as much as it should.

While I continue to pray about this and ask God to help me make it a point to extend hospitality, I'll never reach perfection. And neither will you. We're only human, and we will never get it completely right. But we can keep striving and asking God to show us what He wants our next step to be. Then we can be willing to take that step.

The Next Step in Hospitality

If the idea of hospitality scares you, you don't have to start big. Maybe your next step is just inviting a friend over for coffee or asking that woman who's been on your heart to come over for a piece of pie and good conversation. Or maybe you feel led to host a neighborhood barbecue or to invite the person who has nowhere to go to spend Thanksgiving with your family. I don't know how God is calling you to grow in hospitality, but I do hope you'll say yes, not just for the sake of the people you invite into your home but for your sake also—so you can experience the joy that comes from being an extension of the kind of love Jesus modeled for us.

So, let's be willing to have homes that say *Welcome.* Ones where all who enter know they are loved. Homes that reflect the love of Jesus to every guest who sits at our tables. Let us be the friends and neighbors who put on pots of coffee and offer biblical guidance and empathy to those who are searching. Let us open our doors and, with servants' hearts, see how many people we can encourage, give hope to, and be lights for.

15

Attracting Flies with Honey

Learning to Be the Nice Girl

I used to be a mean girl not that long ago. I'm not proud of it one bit, but it's the truth. I wanted nothing more than to fit in and be liked and accepted, and if that meant gossiping and lying, then so be it. I didn't want to be the mean girl, but I didn't have enough of a backbone to be anything else.

It's not easy being an introvert who is quiet and awkward and doesn't know how to go out and find friends. You and I were designed to desire friendships, and it's lonely being on the outside. How do you find authentic friendships when you are basically the worst at small talk and your insecurity tells you to not even try because no one will like you anyway? What do you do?

Sometimes we are lucky enough to be invited into a group of friends, and sometimes we have to go out and try to find our tribe. While it's a wonderful feeling when we find that group, we also have to make sure it's the right group. We want to find the friendships that breathe life, encouragement, and biblical truth into us. We also want to be that type of friend.

When We Are the Mean Girls

Right after I had our second son, I was invited to a Bible study with several other farm wives from our community. Since we live in a small farm town, it was nice to have other women who understood the struggles, long hours, and uncertainty of this life. It was comforting to have a dedicated group of people with whom to do life.

We leaned on one another in the long seasons of harvest and planting. We made freezer meals, took trips together, babysat one another's children, and were vulnerable with our hearts. We were a close-knit group of Christian women who prayed for and loved on one another, being there when someone needed it.

I let my guard down and was thankful to have finally found somewhere I felt as if I belonged. It was true friendship—the kind where you show up unannounced with a coffee and sit on the bedroom floor for two hours, talking about life. The kind where you can send a text at any hour of the night. The kind where you go to a friend's OB appointment with her and no topic is off-limits in conversation.

So, what does this have to do with me being a mean

girl? Well, those conversations on the bedroom floor were spent gossiping about others in the group. Those late-night texts included tearing down the other women whom we called friends. Bible study was more about condemning who we thought was unworthy than it was about studying the Bible. We hugged women in church on Sunday morning and not more than a few hours later tore them down behind their backs.

If I'm being honest, this is painful to talk about. No part of me wants to tell you these things, but they need to be said. This issue in the church has been swept under the rug for too long, and it needs to be uncovered. I would bet you've felt betrayed or hurt by a Christian woman, and I'd also bet you've done some of the hurting. Part of that is the fact that we are human and make mistakes. Romans 3:23 says we all sin and fall short, but this is a growing trend in the church that far too many women are dealing with daily.

I want this chapter to be about me. Not in a self-centered way. But in the way Jesus admonished in Matthew 7:5: taking the plank out of my own eye so I can help you remove the speck from yours. And how can I help change this problem if I'm not vulnerable enough to share my story with you and show you that I care? So, I'm going to tell my story in hope that it will reach your heart and authentically change the church body.

Every time I sat with those friends and sipped a latte

and let words of jealousy, spite, and condescension come out of my mouth, I ignored the conviction of the Holy Spirit. I ignored everything I knew to be right and true and allowed sin into my life for the sake of community. My desperation and insecurity lived at the forefront of my friendships, and I was sadly willing to be the mean girl in order to be the cool girl.

On the outside, we looked like a good group of Christian women who were living for the Lord. I honestly loved Jesus and wanted to be a good person, just as I believe my friends did. But within the walls of our group were toxic deceit and contrived malice. The nastiness didn't just penetrate those on the outside but also leaked into our own inner circle with secret texts and backhanded comments.

It's so hard to tell this story because it's hard to admit our sins, especially to the world. It feels icky to air our dirty laundry and let people in on the things we wish no one knew. Nothing about this story makes me proud. I type this chapter with tears on my cheeks as I think of the behavior I allowed from myself. If I'm honest with myself, I wasn't okay with my behavior during this season, but I wasn't troubled enough to change it, which is heartbreaking.

First Corinthians 15:33 gives us the truth that says, "Do not be misled: 'Bad company corrupts good character.'" This verse was playing out in my life as I became less concerned with my actions and more able to ignore my conviction of sin.

I still looked like your typical Midwestern Christian good girl, but that was where the problem lay. Almost no one could see the effects of my sin slowly changing and hardening my heart. The game I had been playing was morphing from charade to true character. But I was still the cool girl, people still thought I had this Jesus thing all figured out, and I still shoved away the conviction.

But my husband could see the changes in me. He told me, "You're acting just like them. That's not who you really are. Why won't you stand up for what's right?" He was dead-on, and I knew he was, but I wasn't strong enough to take a stand. I didn't like who I was anymore, but every time I wanted to stand for the truth, I would chicken out for fear of losing my status.

At some point in our lives, we are going to be forced to make a choice and stand for something. There are only so many confrontations we can dance around, so many arguments we can avoid, and so many times we can try to remain neutral to keep everyone happy. At some point, we're going to have to choose.

Finally, I couldn't take it anymore, and neither could Jake. I had to choose to either remain in the in-crowd or stand up for what was right. I struggled to find the words I would say, my heart raced, and my sweaty hands shook. I knew that standing up to one of my dearest friends might not go over well, even if it was done in love. But I also knew that a group of Christian women would realize that what we had been doing was nothing but sin. Evil, hateful, nasty sin. And no one likes to talk about sin.

I felt certain that as a group, we would wake up and realize this and turn from our ways. That we would be true encouragers, no longer backstabbing those whom we said we cared about the most. As I wrestled with what I was going to say, Jake looked at me and said, "You know what the right thing to do is, but you have to grow a backbone and do it. I can't do it for you; you have to choose to do this." The choice I needed to make wrecked me to my very core.

For maybe the first time in my life, I went against the grain. I stood up, even though it came with costly consequences. I spoke the truth in love, but it didn't matter how I said the words if these women weren't ready to hear them. The manipulation, lies, and gossip needed to stop if I was going to call myself a Christian. I couldn't act like this, and our group could no longer go on like this.

I spoke to my best friend about how I felt. In the middle of our conversation, she stormed out, leaving me shocked and confused. I was deleted from our group text and uninvited from the Bible study I had gone to every week with this group of friends. Yes, I was kicked out of Bible study and shunned by every person I thought was a close friend. I was mocked, talked about, and scorned for my actions. I was made the talk of the town because I chose to take a stand, and the irony isn't lost on me that the thing I had done to others was happening to me.

The group of women that I had done life with over the past several years—that had texted me every day, been there for the birth of one of my children, and been a huge support to me—acted as if I no longer existed. They turned against me so fast that my head was left spinning.

Before I knew I'd been shunned by them, I smiled at one of them during preschool pick-up. When my smile was received with a glare, I knew something was off. Not five minutes later, a hateful text came through from that same girl, telling me how ashamed she was of me. That's when I knew I had been deemed an outsider.

Dropped from group texts, uninvited from every event, kicked out of Bible study, and treated as if I no longer existed, all because I went against the grain and stood up for what I believed was right. What happened in that conversation and what my best friend told the group were two very different things. They kicked me to the curb over a lie they believed, with not a single person asking for a second side to the story. I was left standing dumbfounded and heartbroken by the loss of not just one friendship but several.

I'm not alone in that feeling. Almost every one of us has experienced a broken friendship, and the pain runs deep. I have been absolutely shocked by the number of women who have gone through something similar. I've talked to dozens of women who no longer attend church because of the hatefulness they've met within those doors. Women who are put off from relationships with Christ because of members of His church. Because of people like me.

Iron Sharpens Iron

Even though I am no longer friends with these women, I forgave them a long time ago because, honestly, if the roles had been reversed and one of them had stood up against our gossiping ways, I probably would have done the same thing.

And even though that experience was one of the most painful things I've gone through and sometimes the wound still feels raw, it was one of the best things that could have ever happened to me. That loss opened my eyes to the extreme destruction that was happening through our words and actions. Why is it that we have labeled gossip a lesser sin and made excuses as to why it's okay? It's not okay. We don't realize the magnitude of its destruction until we are on the receiving end.

Because I stood for my choice and decided that being the cool girl was no longer worth being the mean girl, I paid a price. I've mourned over lost friendships I truly cared about, but I've realized I have to be accountable for my own actions. I also gained something even more important: an understanding of the damage we are doing with our gossip and other hurtful ways. And now I can try to bring good from this situation and hopefully open the eyes of others who might be doing the same.

It's got to stop, friend. Proverbs 27:17 says, "As iron sharpens iron, so one person sharpens another." God isn't shy when talking about the severity of gossip, slander, and lies, and He goes so far as to call them an abomination (Proverbs 6:16–19, NKJV). James 1:26 says, "Those who consider themselves religious and yet do not keep a tight rein on their tongues deceive themselves, and their religion is worthless." Those words are harsh, but they should alert us to the severity of our actions.

Gossip is never innocent, and no one is ever left unharmed by it. It infects our communities and causes division, and it has zero reward. There is no upside except for the fact that maybe for a few minutes we felt as if we belonged because someone gossiped to us, which we took as a sign that we were accepted and liked.

I know that every woman struggles with this, even—or maybe especially—Christian women. I know that gossip is one of the sins we are most prone to fall into because it doesn't *feel* as if it's that wrong. We compare it with murder or stealing, and really it doesn't look bad at all. And that mindset is exactly the one Satan wants us to have.

He wants us to believe that it isn't *that bad* as we are surrounded by magazines and television shows that promote and thrive on it. But while we are busy justifying and downplaying our sin, calling it venting or going so far as labeling it prayer requests, we are tearing up the hearts of other women. I can't count the number of women who tell me, "The women who have betrayed me or hurt me the most are Christians. I want nothing to do with them."

And they're right. How can I argue with that when I was the person they're talking about and maybe still would be if I hadn't been forced to make a choice? How can I argue with that when countless women are telling me their stories of hurt and betrayal? These are women who have had their spirits crushed and their hearts broken.

Ephesians 4:29 says, "Do not let any unwholesome talk come out of your mouths, but only what is helpful for building others up according to their needs, that it may benefit those who listen." That sets the stage for us. And the very next verse tells us that our slander *grieves* the Holy Spirit. That's big.

We have to take a stand, even if it's uncomfortable. Even if it's awkward and our voices shake. Even if it costs us our friendships. God designed us for relationships, and that includes friendships—but not ones that breed toxicity and sin disguised by Christianity. Is it worth it to fit in if we have to belittle and slander other people to do it? We have to take a stand even if that means pain.

So, can I encourage you today to really look at your heart, no matter how hard it may be to do? Do you struggle with gossip or slander? Are you able to walk away and stand for what is right? I'm not asking whether you're perfect, because the truth is that I've still caught myself in gossip and slander before I even realize it. We're all human. But what is our normal? Do we seek out the juicy details of someone else's life to share, or are we encouragers who use our words to uplift those around us?

If you're finding yourself struggling, I encourage you to keep Psalm 141:3 close as a reminder and prayer. It says, "Set a guard over my mouth, LORD; keep watch over the door of my lips." God wants us to turn from our sin, and He wants us to lean on Him for strength to keep from giving in to our temptation.

I regret so many things about the way I spoke about people, even the people I loved. I can't go back and change those things, but I can do better in the future. I can use my words to encourage others, and I can ask forgiveness for the times I fail. And I can tell you with 100 percent certainty that being the mean girl will absolutely never be worth it to be the cool girl.

16
Keep On Plowing
Learning to Not Give Up

I scrambled to find my phone and silence the blaring alarm before it woke the kids up. Sitting up on the edge of the bed, I rubbed my eyes and tried to give myself a mental pep talk to stand up and get moving. I was thankful I had decided to stay up late the night before to get everything prepared for our thirteen-hour trip. My clothes were laid out, the lunch box full of snacks was packed, the Suburban was loaded with our suitcases, and my coffee cup sat under the Keurig, just waiting for the push of a button.

One by one, I carried the sleeping children to the car, buckled them into their car seats, and tucked their favorite blankets around them. I grabbed my coffee, locked the back door, and slid into the driver's seat. The clock read 2:28 a.m., two minutes ahead of schedule. I turned the radio up as we pulled out of the driveway and tried to mentally prepare for the trip ahead of us.

This was the life of harvest. As we took our combine and other equipment on the road, traveling to several states to harvest other farmers' crops, this was our new normal. We would spend as much time with Jake as possible, usually about two weeks, and I would cook for the crew, run the combine, and make runs for parts when something broke down. We would spend our hours in the combine, cramming in as much time together as a family as possible. Every couple of weeks, we would make the trip back home to check that everything on the farm was still running smoothly.

I was getting used to this back and forth routine. I knew exactly what towns I would need to stop in to get gas, where our favorite fast food places were, and even where the last Starbucks was on our route. There are very few Starbucks in the desolate parts of Nebraska and South Dakota. It's a real shame!

Every time we made this trip, I had hours to sift through my thoughts while the kids slept. I became used to the drive and even looked forward to the solid hours of silence. I thought about how I could so clearly see God moving and shaping our story, and I also thought about how hard this summer had been for our family.

My mind went back and forth, comparing who I was

now with who I once had been. I thought about the ways I had grown in my faith, how my perspective on situations had shifted, and how my heart had been shattered and pieced back together, now stronger than before.

I remembered situation after situation when I felt broken down and defeated, believing I was falling apart through all the pain, tears, and heartache. In the middle of those situations, it seemed as if God had abandoned me, leaving me to wander alone in the wilderness as though He didn't care enough to save me from these trials that seemed to never end.

But oh, how our perspectives change when we are on the other side, when we look back and can so clearly see how God's hand was at work in those darkest moments when we couldn't see Him, when we were not falling apart but instead falling into who He made us to be. We can see how the pain brought strength, the tears brought surrender, and the wilderness brought trust.

Three years before, I don't think I could have handled our family going on harvest as we were now. Back then, I could barely spend two nights away from my husband, let alone weeks. I thought I just wasn't cut out for that kind of sacrifice, and I really didn't want to be in a position to test my ability to handle that kind of situation. I wanted our lives to remain steady, so I tried to use my willpower to keep the boat from rocking and tried to cling to the normalcy I was used to then. The normalcy so easily became an idol.

It's instinctual for us to fear change, even good change, because with change comes the unknown, vulnerability, and a lack of control. It presses us to loosen our grip on our lives and reminds us once again that we aren't the captains of these ships. It reminds us that we don't know the grand scheme of things and we don't always know what is best for us. We rarely do.

So, in the early-morning hours, before dawn tried to break through, I drove through rural Nebraska and dug deep into analyzing how God had brought us to this moment. I was truly in awe of what He had orchestrated that had led us here. The more I dug into my thoughts, the more I became amazed as I looked back and saw the situations and lessons that didn't make sense at the time but were now crystal clear—how each situation had prepared me a little bit more than the last, cultivating strength and perseverance.

I thought about how six months earlier I had prayed for God to shut the door on this opportunity to go across the country to custom harvest if it wasn't His will. I prayed that He would slam the door in our faces. So many times we had been presented with what seemed like an amazing opportunity for our farm, only for it to fall through. I wanted this door to shut before we had the chance to be disappointed. While I knew that custom harvesting could be the thing that got the bankers off our backs, I also knew how hard it would be to make the logistics happen.

I knew how harvest worked. It had always been my favorite time of year on the farm. There is an undeniable and distinct atmosphere that comes with harvest. It's all your hard work and risk coming to fruition as you watch the grain pour into the tank of the combine. It's the smell of wheat dust in the air and the sound of laughter on a picnic blanket as you stop for supper at the edge of the field. It's watching the pure joy on your children's faces as they run through the wheat stubble to greet their dad. Gratitude and reverence penetrate deep into the soul.

But in addition to the joy and thankfulness come eighteen-hour days, high tension, and expensive machinery breakdowns. It's exhaustion, loneliness, and standing at the sink doing dishes at 11:00 p.m., watching the lights of the equipment out in the field and knowing it will still be several hours before the crew calls it quits for the night. It's going nonstop until the crop is in, with no breaks for birthday parties, barbecues, or date nights and without help putting the kids to bed. It's the most intense, exhausting few weeks of the entire year.

The thought of harvest stirs a sense of excitement, fear, joy, and anticipation in most farm families. We breathe sighs of relief when the last load of wheat heads to town and we are ready to start the next season on the farm. The thought of harvest lasting six months instead of a few weeks had brought me to my knees. We would start harvesting in Texas in May and slowly make our way north, all the way to Canada, as the wheat ripened. Every few weeks we would move a little farther north, and that would be our life for over half the year. I'd wondered how we could ever make that work. How could we still take care of our own farm while being gone for so long? How would our kids handle this huge change? How would our marriage hold up under the stress?

Years ago, when facing challenging situations, I begged God to steer us away from them but only because I didn't want to face them. They would have been too hard, too uncomfortable, and I spent hours on my knees, praying for God to give me my way and allow me to avoid the struggle. That was my heart before God used my trials and pain to slowly chip away at my doubts and replace them with faith.

Now I got on my knees and prayed for His will to be done, not just if it suited me but even if it didn't. I prayed with an understanding that I wasn't the one who knew best or could see how the story would play out. I trusted the One who did, even if what He gave me was uncomfortable, because I knew it would be another situation that God could use to change me, to make me more like who He wanted me to be for Him.

God didn't slam the door in our faces. Piece by piece,

everything fell together perfectly. We scrambled to get the equipment ready to leave, to get help lined up to take care of things while we were gone, and to mentally prepare for what we were embarking on in this next season. There was no going back once we started. I promised Jake that no matter how hard it got, I had his back; we were in this together. We were going, even though we were terrified.

Two weeks later, I stood in the driveway, a baby on my hip and two rowdy boys by my side, as we kissed Jake goodbye and told him to be safe. As he pulled out of the driveway, I looked down to see our oldest holding back tears. "It's okay, bud. In a week you'll be done with preschool, and we will get to go with Dad!" I said. He looked at me and said, "Good, Momma, because I can't wait to go on harvest and ride the combine!"

And just like that, the racing of my heart was from excitement instead of fear. This was going to be our hardest summer as a family. We would be tried and tested, repeatedly pushed to our limits, but we knew this was where God wanted us, not because He was leading us along the easy road but because He was handing us an opportunity to serve Him well. He was going to use this summer to mold us like clay in the potter's hands.

Three months into being on the road, we were getting ready for school to start again. We were making as many trips to see Jake as possible, and I tried to juggle all my obligations and priorities smoothly. I was making sure everything got done at the farm, keeping the house running, helping run our store in town, and raising the kids while battling the loneliness of harvest.

I knew this loneliness would sneak in, because it always did during harvest. I was prepared for it, but after three months of my husband's side of the bed being empty, it became more difficult to ignore. I was grateful for Jake's hard work, and I was thankful for the opportunity God had given us. I had pulled up my big-girl panties all summer and done my part. But when we went home and I laid my head down late at night and reached across the bed to an empty pillow, the reminder came that for just a moment I needed to accept my feelings.

I didn't need to pretend I was fine, and I didn't need to act as if my world were crashing down around me. Right there in my lonely middle ground was where God met me. I gave Him my loneliness along with my gratitude. I gave Him my struggles and my wins, my sorrows and my joys. I accepted that it wasn't my strength that was keeping me going; it was His. God knew my good days and bad days, my successes and failures.

Anger and resentment tried to take hold, telling me that our family wasn't strong enough for this. Shame said to suck it up, reminding me that other people have it worse and threatening to invalidate my emotions. Doubt and confusion questioned whether this was really what we were supposed to be doing and what God thought was the best plan for our family. Yet God reminded me of His faithfulness.

I told the anger and resentment that our family didn't need to be strong enough for this because it wasn't our strength we were leaning on when things were hard. I told shame to pack its bags because it was allowed no room in my heart. And I told doubt and confusion that I wasn't the one holding the pen but that I trusted the One who was.

The Right Road Can Still Be Bumpy

It can become so easy to doubt that we are still on the right road when it becomes bumpy. We think that maybe we misread the signs or heard God wrong. When things get hard, it's easy to doubt that we are truly on the path God wants us on. Maybe we even question God's motives.

Marriage gets hard, and we might question whether we married the right person. Being a working mom is hard, and we question whether we are doing the right thing by having a career. We stay at home with our kids, and when money gets tight and we find our days being spent wiping tiny butts and fetching snacks, we question whether we should be working outside the home instead. We look for a different path instead of a way to trust God on the hard road we are walking.

We can forget that God not only calls us to do hard things but also created us to do hard things. Nothing God calls us to will come without its struggles, no matter what it may be or how good it may seem. When we come to a bump in the road, we have to decide whether we are going to press on or turn around and give up. Sometimes giving up sounds like the better option—throwing in the towel and being done with whatever challenge is in front of us. In those moments, I always look to the apostle Paul as an example.

Before Paul came to know Christ, his career was persecuting Christians. But then God got his attention and shook him to his core (see Acts 9:1–19), and he became a man solely after the heart of Jesus on a mission to spread the gospel. It was his one and only goal. His entire life was devoted to sharing the good news, and can you imagine if he would have given up when he came upon roadblocks?

He faced hunger, health issues, multiple imprisonments, stoning, beatings, and death threats (see 2 Corinthians 11:23–27), yet he kept going. His hardships weren't signs that he wasn't following God's will; they were a measure of his faith that *in spite of* these things, he kept marching on in what he had been called to do. He actually rejoiced in his trials and said, "I will boast all the more gladly about my weaknesses, so that Christ's power may rest on me. That is why, for Christ's sake, I delight in weaknesses, in insults, in hardships, in persecutions, in difficulties. For when I am weak, then I am strong" (12:9–10).

Paul understood that it is the power of Christ that keeps us pressing on in our hardships. It allows us to lean on His strength and boast in His power instead of our own. Paul knew that when we are beaten down and worn, it is the perfect opportunity for a display of divine power. We can give it our all yet rest in the knowledge that we aren't in it alone.

Paul said in Galatians 6:9, "Let us not become weary in doing good, for at the proper time we will reap a harvest if we do not give up." He knew that things would get hard for all of us. He knew we would face challenges that would make us want to run the other direction, so he encouraged us to keep going and not give up.

We have to press on, friends. We have to keep going when things get hard and messy and we want to quit. When we think we've reached our breaking point and we are pushed even further, we have to persevere. Our trials aren't for nothing. They stretch us and test us, but they allow God to use us for His holy purpose.

It's hard to see God's purpose when we are in the thick of a hard situation, and sometimes we will never see it this side of heaven. But there are those times when we can look back and see how far God has brought us and how each trial brought out something beautiful in us.

While the journey wasn't necessarily our favorite or maybe we even hated it, we wouldn't be where we are without it.

God Is Not a Passive Observer

The presence of trials does not mean you have stepped outside God's will, and He doesn't sit back on His throne and watch like a passive observer as we face our struggles. He is active in our lives, bringing a holy purpose to our situations and working them for good. He is there to redeem, restore, strengthen, and heal us and to reconcile us to Himself.

What we see as our weaknesses, God sees as opportunities to display the power of Christ. When we think that things have gotten too hard to bear, may we remember that His grace is sufficient and that His power is made perfect in weakness. May we keep pressing on through the trials, through the heartache, and through the pain.

We made it through harvest, and the first night that I lay in my husband's arms in our own bed, I wept sweet tears of relief. I felt as if we had crossed the finish line. We had made it—not without bumps and bruises along the way but with determination, knowing that this season would bring purpose, knowing that God would take it and use it to continue molding us to be more like Him. He would use it to refine us.

As I type this, Jake is outside building fences and finishing the final tasks that need to be done. Tomorrow he will head to Texas to start the harvest season once again, even though it feels as if he just got home. This year, though, I am not afraid. I know that I will face frustration, loneliness, and exhaustion, but I also know that God will be right there with me in every second of it.

And whatever season you may be in that has you questioning God's presence or plan, I pray that you'll keep pressing on during the hard parts. I pray that you will allow His power to work through your weakness and will trust that this season will not go to waste, even if you aren't able to clearly see the purpose yet. God's not done with us, and if we don't give up in whatever it is He has called us to, we will reap the reward.

17

All Our Stories Are Different

Learning to Embrace Where God Has Called You

I picked up the phone, hoping he was still awake. I needed wisdom and guidance, and my dad was the person I knew would set me straight. He answered the phone, and I could tell I hadn't woken him up. "Dad, I need your help. I'm struggling, and I know there is something I'm supposed to be doing. I can't explain this feeling in my gut that I can't shake, but I think God is trying to tell me that I'm supposed to be an author. I'm not a writer, though. I don't have anything to say, and who would even want to read my words? I'm crazy, aren't I?"

I knew that the pause on the other end of the line was him thinking about what advice to bestow on me. I knew that the words I was saying sounded absurd, and I felt as crazy as I sounded. But I couldn't shake the feeling that there was something God was asking me to do. I had never before had this stirring in my soul, and I didn't know how to discern it. It was like trying to find the light switch in a pitch-black room. You know it's there somewhere and you know you're close, but you can't quite find it.

I half hoped my dad would tell me to dream a little more realistically, and I half hoped he would tell me I wasn't crazy. Finally, he said, "Caitlin, you don't have to figure it all out right now; you just need to keep trusting that God will lead you. Why don't you start small and take the first step? Maybe start a blog and just start writing and see where God takes you."

The next day I started the blog, having no idea what I would say or whether anyone would care but tucking that advice from my dad deep into my heart. I wrote what was on my heart but knew next to nothing about the logistics of running a blog. I started and stopped more times than I should have, but that stirring in my soul never left.

When I thought my efforts were for nothing, that feeling in my gut would remind me why I started. I had to ask myself whether I believed the passion in my heart was truly from God and, if it was, whether I trusted Him enough to believe He would bring it to fruition. Did I truly believe all my effort, time, and vulnerability wouldn't go to waste?

Four years later, I called my dad in the middle of the day. "Dad! I have a book deal!" I said between sobs. We both spent a couple of minutes crying on the phone, him out of pride, me out of gratefulness and disbelief. That night I went to my parents' house so I could hug them both and celebrate. "Dad, what if you hadn't told me to be obedient? You're the one who told me to go for it and to trust God. What if you had told me not to chase that dream?" He started to say something, but my mom knew what was coming and handed us both tissues because the waterworks had started again.

The point of this story? The point of this whole book? It isn't to tell you about me or my life. Yes, I've shared so many things with you throughout these pages, but my hope has been that you would know you aren't alone in your struggles. I've shared these memories, triumphs, and valleys with the prayer of telling you God's story. I've told you these things so you might believe that if God can use my story, He can use yours too.

Last spring I drove down the interstate with my dear friend Lauren, who was just getting ready to release her first book. We were chatting about the process of writing a book and the emotions that come with it. She asked me, "What has been a recurring theme you've seen in the book that you didn't expect while writing it?"

I hadn't thought about that, but instantly out of my mouth came the word *redemption*. I looked at her, shocked. "I haven't even thought about that," I said. "But in each story, I just look back and see God's redemption. I see how He loves us enough to redeem the small parts and the big parts of our stories, and I didn't realize that until just this moment."

I laughed at my newfound revelation, and we continued to chat for the rest of our drive. But ever since that word came barreling out of my mouth before my brain had a chance to have a say-so, I cannot stop thinking about just how big God's story of redemption is, not just in my life but in all of ours.

He has given every single one of us a story to tell, but those stories should point back to Him. Every one of us has the opportunity to be used by God to bring Him glory and to show Christ to others through our big moments and through our little ones. Our trials, sins, pain, joys, successes, valleys, and mountaintops are all part of the stories God is writing for us. And whether you think you have a story or not, I promise that you do and that it needs to be told.

Maybe your story is really a thousand little stories woven together, or maybe you have a shattering, life-changing story about when your life's course was altered forever. Either way, you have the choice to tell it. You have the choice to let whatever circumstances you have walked through be a lamp for others. You can be the light that says, "I survived this, and here is how God saw me through."

Your story doesn't look like mine, I'm sure, but that doesn't mean it is any less worthy of being told. Maybe you live in the heart of a big city, or maybe you're in rural America like I am. Maybe your marriage is great, or maybe it's on the brink of destruction. Maybe your family is healthy, or maybe you've lost a child. Whatever your story is, there is one thing I know without a shadow of a doubt: God wants to use it, and He wants to bring beauty from it.

When Moses saw the burning bush and talked to God, he gave excuse after excuse as to why God shouldn't use him. He offered the reasons why he was not up to the task God was giving him: "I'm inadequate; I don't know enough; people won't take me seriously; I'm not good with words; I'm not willing" (see Exodus 3:1–4:17).

His last reason was not an excuse but a statement of the condition of his heart. With every excuse Moses gave, God replied with His promise of provision. That wasn't enough for Moses because the root of the problem was his heart. He lacked the faith and trust to step out in obedience to God, and he asked God to send someone else.

Those five statements have summed up my life so often. Just like with Moses, it always comes down to a heart problem. So many times I have listed off the reasons I could never be a good farm wife, mother, friend, Christian, daughter, sister, author. Each time, though, God kept nudging.

My entire life, I have felt inadequate in every way, yet God has still used me. Every time I compared myself with someone else and felt as if I could never measure up, God still managed to use me. When people mocked my writing and said I should quit, God didn't change His mind about me. All the times I hit Publish and was instantly filled with regret and doubted that my words were good enough, God used those words to reach people.

When I became like Moses and all my excuses failed and my heart condition was exposed, I was left to decide whether I would be willing to go where I was called or whether I would say, "Send someone else."

You might not be called to write, and that's okay. There are thousands of ways we can share our stories with others in the hope of being lights in their darkness. But in case you don't have people to keep you going, as I did, I'm going to be that person for you right now. You know that stirring in your soul that won't go away, that thing you feel called to do that seems too crazy? Dare to be obedient.

Right now you might be saying "Yeah, but I really don't have an exciting story to tell" or "I don't know how I can help anyone by sharing my story." I'm going to tell you two things. One, your story doesn't have to be big or exciting or tragic in order to make an impact, and two, it's not your job to decide how your story helps someone. That part is on God.

Here's the thing: our testimonies aren't about us. They're not about what we did, how we did it, how strong we are, or how awesome we are. They're not supposed to be about us. Our testimonies are about what God has done, not what we have done. They let people know the intimate ways God has moved in our lives and the ways He has transformed us.

Of course, we have to talk about ourselves when we share our testimonies. Throughout these pages, I've told you stories about my farm and family and let you in on so many intimate details of my life. But the point of these pages isn't that you will know me better; it's that you might know God better.

I pray that you've been able to see His goodness and character in a way that maybe you haven't before. Or maybe you know Him well but you needed to be refreshed in hope in your walk of faith. I don't know how God has used these words to reach your heart, but I can tell you I'm thankful that I didn't say, "Send someone else." I'm thankful that I might be a tool that makes even the slightest impact for the kingdom of God.

When I get nervous before speaking at a conference or other event where I will be surrounded by people, I always start questioning my life decisions. That knot drops into my stomach, I feel as if I'm going to pee my pants, and I think, *I'm never doing this again.* My hands start to shake, my heart races, and I have to focus on calming myself down.

Every time that happens, I remind myself of one of my

favorite Bible verses. John 3:30 reads, "He must become greater; I must become less." John the Baptist was testifying that Jesus is the Messiah and that he (John) was just the one who was sent ahead of Jesus. Not only was he willing to step back and recognize his role in God's plan, but he was also downright joyful about it (see verses 28–29).

John could have been jealous of Jesus. He could have been mad that his whole life was devoted to preparing the way for someone greater than he was. Would anyone blame him if he gave the side-eye when he had to tell people he wasn't the Messiah? But John knew it wasn't about him.

When we share our stories, we must share them with the attitude of John the Baptist: with excitement about the opportunity to point people back to Jesus. We have to remember that it's not about us; it's about Him. He must become greater, and we must become less. John trusted that God was writing a bigger story, and he was just thrilled that he got to be part of it.

We get the opportunity to be part of the bigger story. We have the chance to say that we are willing to allow God to use us to show people His love, mercy, kindness, grace, and forgiveness. We can be joyful as we use our stories to point people to the biggest story of them all. We can look back at each lesson we learned in life, and we can be in awe at the way God has used our stories to bring about beauty and joy, even from the messiness and rawness of life.

Washed Clean

I watch my husband crawl out from underneath the tractor, and I see a man so filthy that you would think no shower could ever be hot enough to get him clean. His jeans are covered in dirt from crawling around under the equipment, and his boots are worn and dusty. His ball cap shadows his grease-covered face, and the lines of sweat running down his cheeks leave evidence of the dirt. His calloused hands are blackened from their humble work on that old tractor, and his shirt is ripped from getting snagged on a bolt. He almost looks hopeless.

Then the shower water runs black as the dirt circles the drain. The grease and filth are washed away, revealing the man underneath. A man that looked hopeless is now clean, no trace of dirt left on him. That is what God does with these stories He is writing in our lives. That is the power of God. He takes each chapter from our stories, and instead of leaving us tattered and covered in grime, He makes us clean and new and breathes redemption into the pages. He takes the farmer with his dirt and stains, and He brings out the beauty and joy that were hidden underneath.

Acknowledgments

I stand in awe at all the times I saw God moving to make this book come together. In all my messiness, He never left me. How good He is to always pursue us. He wove everything together in His perfect timing. To God be the glory for it all.

Jake, this book wouldn't have happened without you. So many times I doubted whether this was what I was called to do and even whether God really would equip me to do it. Each time, you lifted my chin, reminded me of who I am, and pushed me to keep going. You never let me quit, and you relentlessly believe in me. You are a servant leader with a heart for Christ, and I could not be more honored to be your wife. Thank you for loving our family so well, for helping keep me near the cross, and for always making my coffee in the morning.

Grady, Porter, and Finley, if I have one prayer for your

lives, it is that you will fearlessly chase after Jesus. I hope each of you believes in yourself as much as I believe in you and that you always know how proud I am of you. Being your momma has taught me so much, and I love being on this adventure with you.

To my parents, Mike and Julie Konkel: I could never find adequate words to express how thankful I am for both of you. Dad, when I called you that night years ago with a wild dream in my heart of one day being an author, you chose to believe that God was calling me and you encouraged me to listen. Thank you. Mom, I couldn't do any of this without you. You selflessly and without hesitation are always there when I need you. You pour out so much of yourself and never ask for anything in return. Thank you both for being a beautiful extension of the gospel and always pointing me to truth.

To my sisters, Cassidy and Madison: Thank you for being such huge supports in my life. You are always there to encourage me and make me laugh. I love you girls, and I love watching you grow in your faith.

To my preacher, Ron Eden: This book probably wouldn't have happened without your encouragement and wisdom. Thank you for believing in these words and never hesitating to remind me of biblical truth. My family is forever grateful for you.

To Terryn, Michaela, Sheila, Brynn, and Becky: Thank you for being my tribe. You are the kind of friends that someone prays for. You never hesitate to speak truth to me, encourage me, and push me off the ledge when I need it. I love you girls.

To Maria: You have been such an incredible influence in my life, and you inspire me to be more like Jesus. You have been an example of what it means to go where God has called, no matter what. Thank you for always pushing me to trust in God and to live fearlessly, believing in who He created me to be. You are a gift to me.

To Bob Hostetler: Thank you for convincing me that I had a story to tell from the farm and for taking a chance on me. I'm forever grateful for your patience, guidance, and wisdom. Thank you also to Steve Laube and the Steve Laube Agency for helping to give this dream life.

To Susan Tjaden: You have been nothing short of amazing to work with, and I'm truly blessed to have you as my editor. Thank you for helping to give my words a home and for being so kind and gracious to this newcomer. You and the team at WaterBrook have made this process so enjoyable, and I am so grateful.